Contents

Choices for Deficit Reduction: An Update

Summary

In coming decades, the aging of the population, rising health care costs, and the expansion of federal subsidies for health insurance will put increasing pressure on the federal budget. At the same time, by 2020, if current laws generally remained in place, federal spending apart from that for Social Security and major health care programs would drop to its smallest percentage of total output in more than 70 years, and federal revenues would be a larger percentage of output than they have been, on average, during the past 40 years.[1] Still, the rising cost of Social Security and the major health care programs would lead to widening deficits, the Congressional Budget Office (CBO) projects. Under those projections, federal debt held by the public would rise substantially over the long term as a share of the economy's annual output—from 72 percent of output now to more than 100 percent of output 25 years from now—which would probably have significant negative consequences for the economy and reduce lawmakers' ability to respond to unexpected developments.

Addressing that long-term challenge would require reducing future budget deficits. To accomplish that, lawmakers would need to increase revenues further relative to the size of the economy, decrease spending on Social Security or major health care programs from what would occur under current law, cut other federal spending to even lower levels by historical standards, or adopt some combination of those approaches. The amount of deficit reduction that would be needed would depend on lawmakers' objectives for federal debt. For example:

- Decreasing that debt in 2038 to just below 70 percent of output—slightly less than what it is now but still quite high by historical standards—could be achieved if deficits were reduced by $2 trillion (excluding interest costs) during the next decade, and the reduction in the deficit as a percentage of output in 2023 was maintained in later years.

- Lowering the debt in 25 years to about 30 percent of output—which would be a little below the average over the past 40 years—could be achieved by reducing deficits by $4 trillion (excluding interest costs) during the next decade and maintaining that reduction in subsequent years.

Achieving savings of $2 trillion or more during the next 10 years would require significant increases in taxes, significant cuts in federal benefits or services, or both.

Making the task of deficit reduction more complicated is the economy's slow recovery from the severe recession. By CBO's estimate, the economy is now about 5 million jobs short of where it would be if the unemployment rate was down to its sustainable level and participation in the labor force was back up to its trend. The shortage of jobs has occurred mostly because demand for goods and services has been weak relative to the productive capacity of the economy. That shortfall in demand has stemmed largely from the lingering effects of the housing bubble and financial crisis. Also contributing, however, has been the most abrupt fiscal tightening that has occurred since the end of World War II, as the federal deficit shrank from about 10 percent of gross domestic product (GDP) in fiscal year 2009 to about 4 percent in 2013. Although that tightening has had the beneficial effect of slowing the accumulation of federal debt, it also has slowed economic growth during the past few years. Thus, lawmakers face difficult trade-offs when deciding how quickly to carry out policy changes that would make the path of federal debt more sustainable.

---

1. In this document, "the past 40 years" refers to the period from 1973 to 2012.

This report reviews the scale and sources of the federal government's budgetary imbalance, various options for bringing spending and taxes into closer alignment, and criteria that lawmakers and the public might use to evaluate different approaches to deficit reduction. The discussion draws from CBO's *Options for Reducing the Deficit: 2014 to 2023* (November 2013) and serves as an update to the publication *Choices for Deficit Reduction* (November 2012).[2]

The analysis in this report is based on CBO's most recent 10-year budget projections, which were issued in May, and on the agency's long-term budget projections, which were issued in September. The analysis does not include the effect of the recently passed Bipartisan Budget Act of 2013. Over the next 10 years, the agency estimates, that legislation would decrease mandatory spending by $78 billion, increase revenues by $7 billion, and increase discretionary spending by $63 billion if appropriations during the next decade equaled the limits set in current law rather than the limits set in prior law.

How Big Are Projected U.S. Deficits and Debt?

Between 2009 and 2012, the federal government recorded the largest budget deficits relative to the size of the economy since 1946, causing federal debt to soar. At 72 percent of GDP, federal debt held by the public is now higher than it has been at any point in U.S. history except for a brief period toward the end of World War II and a few years after; and it is twice the percentage recorded at the end of 2007. If current laws generally remained in place—an assumption underlying CBO's baseline projections—federal debt held by the public would decline slightly relative to GDP over the next several years.[3] After that, however, growing deficits would ultimately push debt back above its current high level,

in CBO's estimation. In 2038, CBO projects, federal debt held by the public would reach 100 percent of GDP—more than in any year except 1945 and 1946—even without accounting for the harmful effects that growing debt would have on the economy; taking those effects into account boosts projected debt to 108 percent of GDP.

How Are Major Components of the Budget Changing Over Time?

If current laws remained unchanged, Social Security and the federal government's major health care programs would absorb a much larger share of the economy's total output in the future than they have in the past. Projected increases would stem from three factors: the aging of the population; rising health care spending per beneficiary; and changes related to the Affordable Care Act (ACA), specifically the introduction of exchange subsidies and the expansion of Medicaid in many states.[4] Meanwhile, by 2020, spending for all other federal activities would account for its smallest share of GDP in more than 70 years. Taking those pieces together, total federal spending other than interest on the debt would be greater relative to the size of the economy than it has been, on average, during the past 40 years.

At the same time, under current law, revenues would represent a larger percentage of GDP in the future than they generally have in the past few decades. However, CBO projects that revenues would not keep pace with outlays, so deficits would rise and federal debt would grow at a faster pace than the overall economy.

What Are the Consequences of Large and Growing Federal Debt?

Because federal debt is already unusually high relative to GDP, further increases in that debt could be especially harmful. How long the nation could sustain the projected growth in federal debt relative to the size of the economy is impossible to predict with any confidence. At some point, investors would begin to doubt the government's willingness or ability to pay U.S. debt obligations, making it more difficult or more expensive for the government to borrow money.

---

2. See Congressional Budget Office, *Options for Reducing the Deficit: 2014 to 2023*, www.cbo.gov/publication/44715, and Congressional Budget Office, *Choices for Deficit Reduction* (November 2012), www.cbo.gov/publication/43692.

3. CBO's baseline projections are meant to serve as a benchmark for measuring the budgetary effects of proposed changes to federal revenues or spending. They are not meant to be predictions of future budgetary outcomes; rather, they represent CBO's best judgment about how the economy and other factors would affect revenues and spending if current law did not change. By generally following current law, CBO's baselines incorporate the assumption that some policy changes that lawmakers have routinely made in the past—such as preventing the sharp cuts to Medicare's payment rates for physicians called for by law—would not be made again.

4. As referred to in this report, the Affordable Care Act comprises the Patient Protection and Affordable Care Act, the health care provisions of the Health Care and Education Reconciliation Act of 2010, and the effects of subsequent related judicial decisions, statutory changes, and administrative actions.

Moreover, even before that point was reached, the high and rising amount of federal debt that CBO projects would have significant negative consequences for both the economy and the federal budget. Higher debt would lead to larger interest payments; making those payments would eventually require some combination of lower noninterest spending and higher taxes. In addition, increases in debt tend to reduce national saving, leading to more borrowing from abroad and less domestic investment, which in turn reduces people's future income relative to what it would otherwise be. Also, when debt rises, lawmakers are less able to use tax and spending policies to respond to unexpected challenges, such as economic downturns or international crises. Rising debt could itself precipitate a fiscal crisis by undermining investors' confidence in the government's ability to manage the budget.

What Policy Changes Could Lower the Trajectory of Federal Debt?

Lawmakers could set various goals for deficit reduction and the trajectory of debt. If current laws generally remained in place, deficits would total about $6 trillion over the next 10 years and debt would reach 108 percent of GDP by 2038, CBO projects. Alternatively, for example, with gradually increasing amounts of deficit reduction totaling $2 trillion over the next 10 years (excluding effects on interest payments and with the reduction as a percentage of GDP in 2023 maintained in later years), federal debt held by the public would drop to 61 percent of GDP in fiscal year 2023 before rising again to 67 percent in 2038. Or, as another example, with gradually increasing amounts of deficit reduction totaling $4 trillion over the next decade, debt would drop to 51 percent of GDP in fiscal year 2023 and decline even further, to 31 percent, by 2038.

To put the federal budget on either of those paths, lawmakers would need to make significant policy changes—allowing revenues to rise substantially more than would occur under current law, reducing spending for large benefit programs to amounts considerably below those currently projected, or adopting some combination of those approaches. Although changes in other activities of the federal government could affect the magnitude of the changes needed to policies that govern taxes or large benefit programs, they could not eliminate the basic trade-off that exists between those two parts of the budget.

What Criteria Might Be Used to Evaluate Policy Changes?

When considering policy changes that would reduce budget deficits, lawmakers and the public might want to consider several factors: How much deficit reduction is appropriate? What is the proper size of the federal government and the best way to allocate federal resources? What types of policy changes would most enhance prospects for near-term and long-term economic growth? What would be the distributional implications of proposed changes—that is, who would bear the burden of particular cuts in spending or increases in taxes, and who would realize long-term economic benefits? The way that people think about those criteria, and the relative importance they attach to different criteria, will vary according to their individual preferences and priorities.

How Big Are Projected U.S. Deficits and Debt?

The economy's gradual recovery from the 2007–2009 recession, the waning budgetary effects of policies enacted in response to the weak economy, and other changes to tax and spending policies caused the deficit to shrink in fiscal year 2013 to its smallest size relative to the economy since 2008—about 4 percent of GDP, compared with a peak of almost 10 percent in 2009. In CBO's 10-year baseline budget projections, which incorporate the assumption that current laws generally remain in place, the deficit is projected to continue to drop over the next few years, falling to 2 percent of GDP by 2015. If that happened, by 2018, federal debt held by the public would decline to 68 percent of GDP from its current level of 72 percent (see Table 1).[5]

---

5. For details about CBO's most recent 10-year baseline, see Congressional Budget Office, *Updated Budget Projections: Fiscal Years 2013 to 2023* (May 2013), www.cbo.gov/publication/44172. In July 2013, the Bureau of Economic Analysis (BEA) revised upward the historical values for GDP; until CBO produces its next economic forecast, it is simply extrapolating those revisions when projecting outcomes as a percentage of future GDP. Thus, although CBO's projections of federal revenues, outlays, deficits, and debt over the 2013–2023 period have not changed since the baseline projections were issued in May, those amounts measured as a percentage of GDP are now lower as a result of BEA's revisions. See Congressional Budget Office, "CBO's Baseline Budget Projections, as of May 2013, With Percentages of GDP Updated to Reflect Recent Revisions by the Bureau of Economic Analysis" (September 2013), www.cbo.gov/publication/44574; also see "Historical Budget Data—August 2013" (August 2013), www.cbo.gov/publication/44507.

Table 1.

Deficits Projected in CBO's Baseline

	Actual, 2013[a]	2014	2015	2016	2017	2018	2019	2020	2021	2022	2023	Total 2014-2018	Total 2014-2023
						In Billions of Dollars							
Revenues	2,774	3,042	3,399	3,606	3,779	3,943	4,103	4,280	4,494	4,732	4,959	17,769	40,336
Outlays	3,454	3,602	3,777	4,038	4,261	4,485	4,752	5,012	5,275	5,620	5,855	20,163	46,677
Deficit	**-680**	**-560**	**-378**	**-432**	**-482**	**-542**	**-648**	**-733**	**-782**	**-889**	**-895**	**-2,394**	**-6,340**
Debt Held by the Public at the End of the Year	11,982	12,685	13,156	13,666	14,223	14,827	15,537	16,330	17,168	18,118	19,070	n.a.	n.a.
						As a Percentage of Gross Domestic Product							
Revenues	16.7	17.7	18.6	18.5	18.3	18.2	18.1	18.1	18.2	18.4	18.5	18.3	18.3
Outlays	20.8	20.9	20.7	20.8	20.6	20.7	21.0	21.2	21.4	21.8	21.8	20.7	21.1
Deficit	**-4.1**	**-3.3**	**-2.1**	**-2.2**	**-2.3**	**-2.5**	**-2.9**	**-3.1**	**-3.2**	**-3.5**	**-3.3**	**-2.5**	**-2.9**
Debt Held by the Public at the End of the Year	72.1	73.6	72.1	70.3	68.8	68.4	68.6	69.0	69.6	70.4	71.1	n.a.	n.a.

Sources: Congressional Budget Office; Department of the Treasury.

Notes: These data reflect recent revisions by the Bureau of Economic Analysis to estimates of gross domestic product (GDP) in past years and CBO's extrapolation of those revisions to projected future GDP.

n.a. = not applicable.

a. Amounts for 2013 were derived from information reported in Department of the Treasury, *Final Monthly Treasury Statement of Receipts and Outlays of the United States Government for Fiscal Year 2013 Through September 30, 2013, and Other Periods* (October 2013), www.fms.treas.gov/mts/mts0913.pdf.

However, deficits would gradually rise again under current law, CBO projects. Interest rates are expected to rebound from their current unusually low levels, sharply increasing the cost of paying interest on the government's debt. Moreover, the pressures created by an aging population, rising health care costs, and an expansion of federal subsidies for health insurance are projected to cause spending for the largest benefit programs to rise as a percentage of GDP after 2018. In addition, CBO projects, revenues would gradually decline relative to GDP for several years after 2015 as receipts from corporate income taxes and remittances from the Federal Reserve diminished as a share of the economy. By 2023, under current law, the budget deficit is projected to total 3.3 percent of GDP. In that year, federal debt would equal 71 percent of GDP and would be rising relative to the size of the economy.

The long-term prospects for the budget are more worrisome. Looking beyond the 10-year period covered by its regular baseline projections, CBO has produced an extended baseline that extrapolates those projections through 2038 (and, with even greater uncertainty, through later decades).[6] The gap between federal spending and revenues is projected to widen steadily after 2015 (see Figure 1), CBO projects; by 2038, the deficit would be 6½ percent of GDP, larger than in any year between 1947 and 2008.[7] With such large deficits, federal debt would be rising significantly faster than GDP, a path that

---

6. See Congressional Budget Office, *The 2013 Long-Term Budget Outlook* (September 2013), www.cbo.gov/publication/44521. CBO's long-term projections generally adhere closely to current law, following the agency's May 2013 baseline budget projections through 2023 and then extending the baseline concept into later years; hence, they are referred to as the extended baseline.

7. Budgetary values after 2023 are presented as percentages of GDP rounded to the nearest one-half percent.

Figure 1.

Federal Debt, Spending, and Revenues Under CBO's Extended Baseline

(Percentage of gross domestic product)

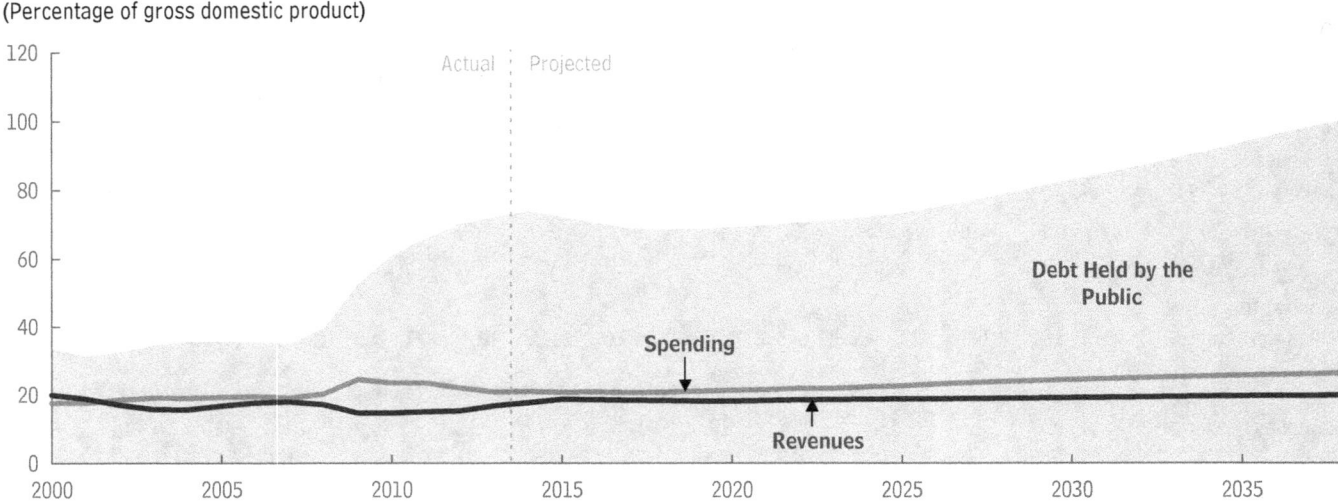

Source: Congressional Budget Office.

Notes: The extended baseline generally adheres closely to current law, following CBO's 10-year baseline budget projections through 2023 and then extending the baseline concept for the rest of the long-term projection period. The long-term projections of debt shown here do not reflect the economic effects of the policies underlying the extended baseline. See Congressional Budget Office, *The 2013 Long-Term Budget Outlook* (September 2013), www.cbo.gov/publication/44521.

These numbers reflect recent revisions by the Bureau of Economic Analysis to estimates of gross domestic product (GDP) in past years and CBO's extrapolation of those revisions to projected future GDP. See Congressional Budget Office, "CBO's Baseline Budget Projections, as of May 2013, With Percentages of GDP Updated to Reflect Recent Revisions by the Bureau of Economic Analysis" (September 2013), www.cbo.gov/publication/44574; also see "Historical Budget Data—August 2013" (August 2013), www.cbo.gov/publication/44507.

Numbers for 2013 were derived from information reported in Department of the Treasury, *Final Monthly Treasury Statement of Receipts and Outlays of the United States Government for Fiscal Year 2013 Through September 30, 2013, and Other Periods* (October 2013), www.fms.treas.gov/mts/mts0913.pdf.

would ultimately be unsustainable. Federal debt held by the public would reach 100 percent of GDP by 2038—even without factoring in the harm that growing debt would cause to the economy (see Figure 2). Taking into account such effects, CBO projects that debt would reach 108 percent of GDP, more than in any year except 1945 and 1946.

If tax and spending policies differed significantly from those specified in current law, budgetary outcomes could differ substantially as well. To illustrate the extent of such differences, CBO analyzed the effects of some additional sets of fiscal policies. Under one set of alternative policies, referred to as the extended alternative fiscal scenario, certain policies that are now in place but scheduled to change under current law would continue instead, and some provisions of current law that might be difficult to sustain for a long period would be modified.[8] Under that scenario, deficits (excluding the government's interest

costs) would be a total of about $2 trillion higher over the next decade than in CBO's 10-year baseline; in subsequent years, deficits would exceed those projected in the extended baseline by rapidly growing amounts. Federal debt held by the public would reach 81 percent of GDP in 2023 and 190 percent by 2038, CBO projects.

How Are Major Components of the Budget Changing Over Time?

The upward pressure on federal spending relative to the size of the economy is attributable not to general growth in the size of the federal government but to growth in just

---

8.   For more detail about the extended alternative fiscal scenario, see Congressional Budget Office, *The 2013 Long-Term Budget Outlook* (September 2013), p. 84, www.cbo.gov/publication/44521.

Figure 2.

Federal Debt Held by the Public Under CBO's Extended Baseline

(Percentage of gross domestic product)

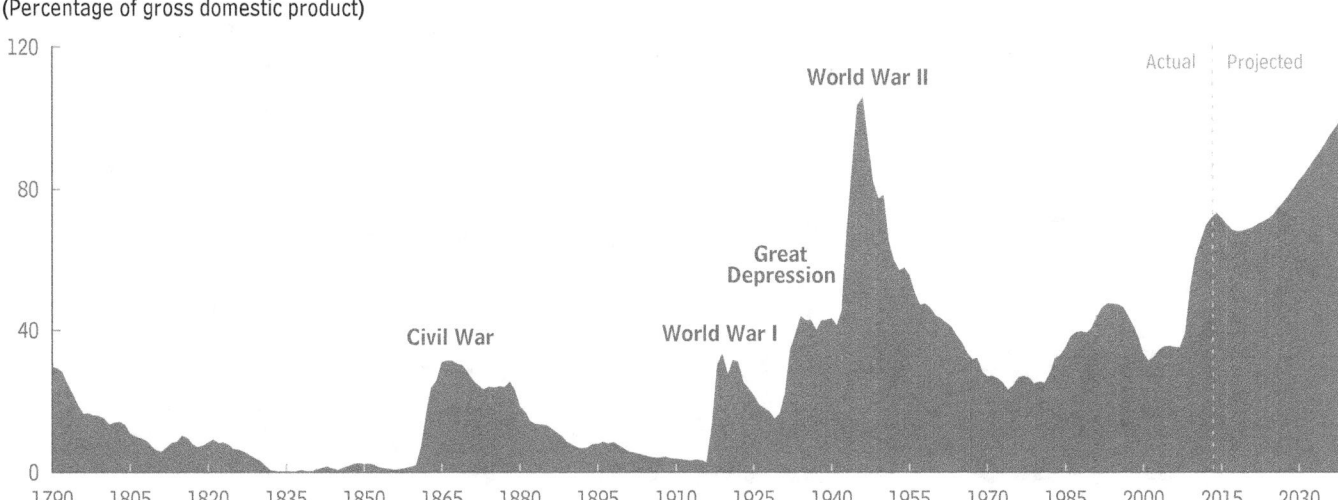

Source: Congressional Budget Office.

Notes: For details about the sources of data used for past debt held by the public, see Congressional Budget Office, "Historical Data on Federal Debt Held by the Public" (July 2010), www.cbo.gov/publication/21728.

The extended baseline generally adheres closely to current law, following CBO's 10-year baseline budget projections through 2023 and then extending the baseline concept for the rest of the long-term projection period. The long-term projections of debt shown here do not reflect the economic effects of the policies underlying the extended baseline. See Congressional Budget Office, *The 2013 Long-Term Budget Outlook* (September 2013), www.cbo.gov/publication/44521.

Data from 1929 onward reflect recent revisions by the Bureau of Economic Analysis to estimates of gross domestic product (GDP) in past years and CBO's extrapolation of those revisions to projected future GDP.

Numbers for 2013 were derived from information reported in Department of the Treasury, *Final Monthly Treasury Statement of Receipts and Outlays of the United States Government for Fiscal Year 2013 Through September 30, 2013, and Other Periods* (October 2013), www.fms.treas.gov/mts/mts0913.pdf.

a handful of the largest programs—Social Security and major health care programs, primarily Medicare, Medicaid, and subsidies provided through new health insurance exchanges. Projected increases would stem from three factors: the aging of the population; the expansion of federal support for health insurance under the ACA; and rising health care spending per beneficiary.

Without significant changes in the laws governing those large benefit programs, those factors would keep federal outlays as a percentage of GDP above the average of the past 40 years, even though spending in other broad categories of the budget is projected to decline relative to GDP (see Figure 3).[9] That conclusion applies under any plausible predictions of future trends in

demographics, economic conditions, and health care costs. Under current law, the increase in spending for those programs relative to GDP would not be matched by a corresponding increase in revenues, even though revenues are expected to rise significantly above their historical average percentage of GDP.

Spending for Social Security

The cost of the Social Security program will rise significantly in coming decades—a development that analysts have long foreseen. The aging of the population is the main factor driving the projected growth of Social Security spending as a percentage of GDP. As more members of the baby-boom generation reach retirement age and as longer life spans lead to longer retirements, a significantly larger share of the population will draw Social Security benefits. In addition, average benefits per beneficiary tend to grow over time because the earnings on which those benefits are based also increase.

---

9. The 40-year average covers a period of diverse economic and fiscal activity and is the benchmark that CBO generally uses when describing budgetary trends. However, other time frames can also provide valid benchmarks.

Figure 3.

Spending and Revenues Under CBO's Baseline, Compared With Past Averages

(Percentage of gross domestic product)

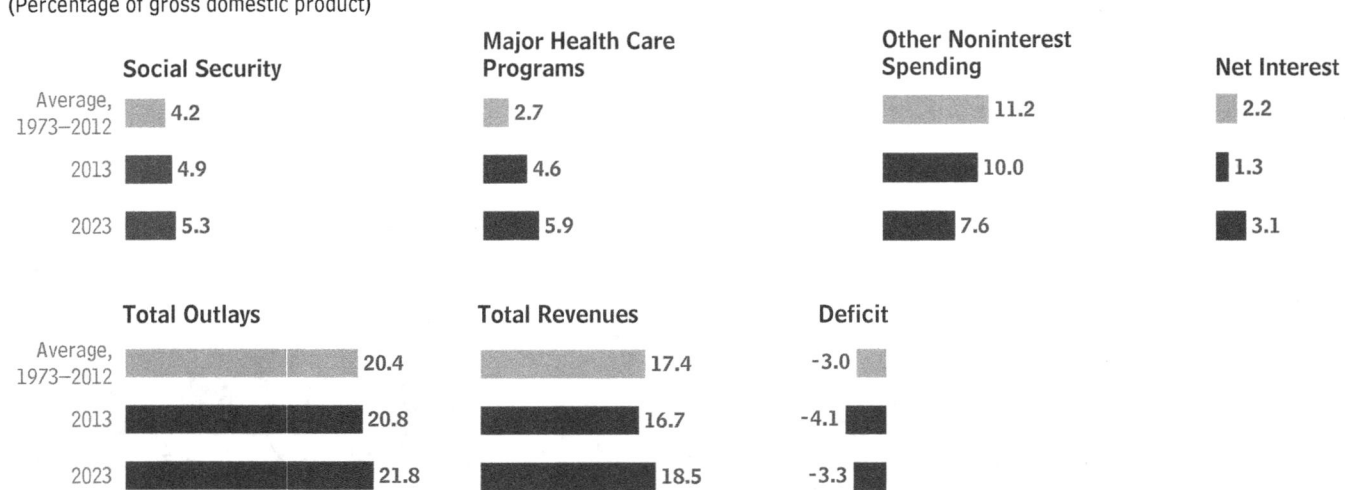

Source: Congressional Budget Office.

Notes: These numbers reflect recent revisions by the Bureau of Economic Analysis (BEA) to estimates of gross domestic product (GDP) in past years and CBO's extrapolation of those revisions to projected future GDP. Although CBO's projections of outlays, revenues, and deficits for 2023 have not changed since they were issued in May, those amounts measured as a percentage of GDP are now lower as a result of BEA's revisions. See Congressional Budget Office, "CBO's Baseline Budget Projections, as of May 2013, With Percentages of GDP Updated to Reflect Recent Revisions by the Bureau of Economic Analysis" (September 2013), www.cbo.gov/publication/ 44574; also see "Historical Budget Data—August 2013" (August 2013), www.cbo.gov/publication/44507.

Numbers for 2013 were derived from information reported in Department of the Treasury, *Final Monthly Treasury Statement of Receipts and Outlays of the United States Government for Fiscal Year 2013 Through September 30, 2013, and Other Periods* (October 2013), www.fms.treas.gov/mts/mts0913.pdf.

Major health care programs consist of Medicare, Medicaid, the Children's Health Insurance Program, and subsidies offered through new health insurance exchanges and related spending. (Medicare spending is net of offsetting receipts.) Other noninterest spending is all federal spending other than that for major health care programs, Social Security, and net interest.

According to CBO's projections, the number of people age 65 or older will increase by 37 percent over the next decade. Accordingly, spending for Social Security is expected to total 5.3 percent of GDP in 2023, compared with 4.9 percent in 2013 and an average of 4.2 percent over the past four decades. CBO estimates that more than four-fifths of Social Security spending in 2023 would go toward benefits for retired workers and their dependents and survivors; the remainder would go toward benefits for disabled workers and their spouses and children.

Spending for Major Health Care Programs

Although spending for health care in the United States has grown more slowly in recent years than it had previously, high and rising levels of such spending continue to pose a budgetary challenge. Outlays for the federal government's major health care programs—Medicare, Medicaid, the Children's Health Insurance Program (CHIP), and subsidies provided through new health insurance exchanges and related spending—are projected

to total 5.9 percent of GDP in 2023, up from 4.6 percent in 2013 and an average of 2.7 percent over the past 40 years.[10]

The increase in spending for health care programs is projected to be much greater than the increase for Social Security because the increase for the health care programs stems not just from the aging of the population, but also from the expansion of federal support for health insurance (which will boost the number of Medicaid recipients

---

10. CBO and the staff of the Joint Committee on Taxation (JCT) estimate that the provisions of the ACA that expand health insurance coverage will have a net cost equal to 0.6 percent of GDP in 2023. See *Effects on Health Insurance and the Federal Budget for the Insurance Coverage Provisions in the Affordable Care Act—May 2013 Baseline*, www.cbo.gov/publication/44190. Under the ACA, reductions in other federal spending and other increases in revenues will slightly offset the net cost of the coverage provisions, yielding a net reduction in the deficit, according to CBO's and JCT's estimates.

and make other people eligible for subsidies for health insurance purchased through exchanges) and from rising costs per beneficiary. In particular, CBO expects that per capita spending on health care will continue to grow faster than per capita spending on other goods and services for many years. On average, between 1985 and 2011, the nation's overall health care costs per person grew about 1½ percentage points faster per year than potential GDP per person (where potential GDP is the maximum sustainable output of the economy) after removing the effects of demographic changes. In projecting future costs, CBO anticipates that the difference between those two growth rates will be smaller than its average of recent decades.[11] Nevertheless, the government's spending for health care per beneficiary is projected to grow sharply under current law.

Despite the significant expansion of federal support for health care for lower-income people enacted in the ACA, about three-fifths of spending for major health care programs in 2023 would finance care for people over age 65, CBO projects. Another one-fifth would finance health care for blind and disabled people, and the remaining one-fifth would finance care for able-bodied, nonelderly people.

Other Spending for Benefits and Services
Besides Social Security and major health care programs, the federal government spends money on a wide variety of benefits and services, including national defense, income security programs, retirement benefits for federal civilian employees and military personnel, transportation, health research, education, law enforcement, agriculture, and many other activities. Those programs and services encompass activities funded through annual appropriations—known as discretionary spending—and activities for which spending is generally determined by setting eligibility rules and benefit formulas—known as mandatory spending. Unlike spending for Social Security and major health care programs, spending on all of those other activities is projected to decline considerably relative to the size of the economy over the next 10 years if current law remains unchanged. Taken together, outlays for that broad collection of other programs and activities would equal 7.6 percent of GDP in 2023, compared with an

average of 11.2 percent over the past 40 years.[12] In fact, by 2020, such spending would decline to a smaller percentage of GDP than has been seen for more than 70 years.

Thus, the United States is already on track to significantly shrink the federal resources dedicated to activities other than Social Security, the major health care programs, and interest on the debt to a much smaller share of the economy than they have represented for the past several decades. Such reductions might prove unpopular once they took effect or, in the case of discretionary programs, once policymakers determined the amount of funding to allocate to specific benefits and services. As a result, those reductions might be difficult to carry out and maintain.

Net Interest
CBO expects interest rates to rebound in coming years from their current unusually low levels. As a result, the government's net interest costs are projected to more than double relative to the size of the economy over the next 10 years—from 1.3 percent of GDP in 2013 to more than 3 percent by 2023—even though, under current law, federal debt is expected to be slightly smaller relative to GDP in 2023 than it is today.

Total Outlays
According to CBO's projections, the substantial decline in other federal spending relative to GDP would not be enough to offset the increased burden placed on the budget by rising outlays for Social Security, major health care programs, and interest payments. Putting those pieces together, CBO projects that total outlays under current law would equal 21.8 percent of GDP in 2023, compared with an average of 20.4 percent since 1973.

Revenues
Federal revenues are expected to rise significantly above levels experienced in recent years; however, that projected increase would not be sufficient to keep pace with the projected increase in federal outlays. After amounting to

---

11. For details about how CBO calculated that difference in growth rates during the past 25 years and the factors affecting the growth in health care spending, see Congressional Budget Office, *The 2013 Long-Term Budget Outlook* (September 2013), pp. 38–42, www.cbo.gov/publication/44521.

12. Defense spending accounts for a little more than one-third of the outlays for that category. Over the past four decades, outlays for defense have averaged 4.5 percent of GDP (they declined from 5.7 percent of GDP in 1973 to 2.9 percent between 1999 and 2001 and then rose to a peak of 4.7 percent in 2010). The caps on funding set by the Budget Control Act of 2011 would cause defense spending to grow more slowly than the economy, leaving total outlays for defense at 2.6 percent of GDP in 2023, CBO projects.

nearly 18 percent of GDP in 2007, federal revenues fell sharply in 2009, to less than 15 percent of GDP—primarily because of the severe recession—and remained close to that percentage through 2011. Revenues grew to 16.7 percent of GDP in 2013 because the economy improved and changes in certain tax rules resulted in higher tax rates.[13]

By 2015, CBO projects, revenues would reach 18.6 percent of GDP, spurred by the ongoing economic recovery and scheduled changes in provisions of tax law (such as the expiration at the end of December 2013 of enhanced depreciation deductions). Under current law, revenues are expected to decline a bit as a share of GDP for a few years after 2015 and then rise again, reaching 18.5 percent in 2023—higher than their 40-year average of 17.4 percent of GDP but still well below projected spending in that year.

Revenues would be greater if not for the more than 200 tax expenditures in the individual and corporate income tax systems and the payroll tax system, which totaled more than $1 trillion in 2013, CBO estimates.[14] Those tax expenditures—so called because they resemble federal spending by providing financial assistance for specific activities, entities, or groups of people—are exclusions, deductions, exemptions, preferential tax rates, and credits that cause revenues to be lower than they would be otherwise for any given schedule of tax rates.

Ten of the largest tax expenditures accounted for approximately two-thirds of the total budgetary effect of all tax expenditures in 2013, CBO estimates. Those 10 large expenditures fall into four major categories:

■ *Exclusions* from taxable income of employment-based health insurance, net pension contributions and earnings, capital gains on assets transferred at death, and a portion of Social Security and Railroad Retirement benefits;

■ *Itemized deductions* for certain taxes paid to state and local governments, mortgage interest payments, and charitable contributions;

■ *Preferential tax rates* applied to capital gains and dividends; and

■ *Tax credits*, specifically the earned income tax credit and the child tax credit.

CBO estimates that in 2013 those 10 tax expenditures accounted for more than $900 billion in forgone revenues from income and payroll taxes, or 5.6 percent of GDP, and they are projected to amount to nearly $12 trillion, or 5.3 percent of GDP, between 2014 and 2023. In 2013, CBO estimates, the combined costs of the 10 tax expenditures equaled about one-third of federal revenues, and they exceeded spending on Social Security, Medicare, or defense.

Beginning in 2014, the refundable tax credits that some people will receive under the ACA to help pay health insurance premiums will represent a new tax expenditure. CBO and the staff of the Joint Committee on Taxation (JCT) estimate that the combined effect on revenues and outlays from those credits would equal 0.2 percent of GDP in 2015 and 0.5 percent of GDP by 2023.

What Are the Consequences of Large and Growing Federal Debt?

How long the nation could sustain growth in federal debt relative to the size of the economy is impossible to predict with any confidence. At some point, investors would begin to doubt the government's willingness or ability to pay U.S. debt obligations, making it more difficult or more expensive for the government to borrow money. Moreover, even before that point was reached, the high and rising amount of debt that CBO projects under the extended baseline would have significant negative consequences for both the economy and the federal budget:

■ Increased borrowing by the federal government would eventually reduce private investment in productive capital because the portion of total savings used to buy government securities would not be available to finance private investment. The result would be a

---

13. In January 2013, payroll tax rates rose with the expiration of a temporary 2 percentage-point reduction in effect for 2011 and 2012, and the top income tax rate rose from 35 percent to 39.6 percent for single taxpayers with income above $400,000 and for married taxpayers with income above $450,000 who file joint returns.

14. The estimates of tax expenditures account for effects both from income taxes and from payroll taxes. Because they are based on people's behavior under current tax law, the estimates do not represent the revenues the government would collect if those provisions of the tax code were eliminated and taxpayers adjusted their activities in response. See Congressional Budget Office, *The Distribution of Major Tax Expenditures in the Individual Income Tax System* (May 2013), www.cbo.gov/publication/43768.

smaller stock of capital and lower output and income in the long run than would otherwise be the case. Despite those reductions, the continued growth of productivity would make real (inflation-adjusted) output and income per person higher in the future than they are now.

- Federal spending on interest payments would rise, thus requiring more substantial changes in tax and spending policies to achieve any chosen targets for budget deficits and debt.

- The government would have less flexibility to use tax and spending policies to respond to unexpected challenges, such as economic downturns or wars.

- The risk of a fiscal crisis—in which investors demanded very high interest rates to finance the government's borrowing needs—would increase.[15]

What Policy Changes Could Lower the Trajectory of Federal Debt?

The large amount of debt that the government has already accumulated and the long-term growth in that debt that CBO projects in its extended baseline present lawmakers and the public with difficult choices. To put federal debt on a significantly lower trajectory, lawmakers would need to change policies in at least one of the following ways:

- Make major reductions in spending for the largest federal benefit programs relative to what would occur under current law; or

- Raise federal revenues substantially, boosting them even further above their historical average percentage of GDP than the amounts that would be collected under current law.

Changes in spending for other activities of the federal government—which, by the end of this decade and beyond, is projected to equal a smaller share of GDP than it did in 1940—could affect the magnitude of the changes needed in taxes or large benefit programs, but

they would not eliminate the need to make significant changes in at least one of those two parts of the budget.

Possible Targets and Approaches for Deficit Reduction

Under CBO's extended baseline, and incorporating the effects of rising debt on the economy, federal debt held by the public would reach 108 percent of GDP by 2038. To lower the trajectory of federal debt, lawmakers could set various deficit reduction goals. CBO projects that deficits under current law would total $6.3 trillion over the next 10 years. Different amounts of deficit reduction during that decade and in later years would put debt on different trajectories (see Figure 4). For example:

- With gradually increasing amounts of deficit reduction totaling $2 trillion from 2014 through 2023 (excluding savings in interest payments), debt would drop to 61 percent of GDP in fiscal year 2023. If the reduction in the deficit as a percentage of output in 2023 was maintained in later years, debt would increase again to 67 percent of GDP by 2038.

- With gradually increasing amounts of deficit reduction totaling $4 trillion from 2014 through 2023 (excluding savings in interest payments), debt would drop to 51 percent of GDP in fiscal year 2023. If the reduction in the deficit as a percentage of output in 2023 was maintained in later years, debt would decline even further to 31 percent of GDP by 2038.[16]

To provide some perspective about the scope and scale of policy changes that would be necessary to put debt on a significantly lower trajectory than would occur under current law, this section presents various options that involve three broad budget categories—mandatory spending, discretionary spending, and revenues. The

---

15. For more details, see Congressional Budget Office, *Federal Debt and the Risk of a Fiscal Crisis* (July 2010), www.cbo.gov/ publication/21625.

16. For additional details on the economic and budgetary effects of those two paths, see *The 2013 Long-Term Budget Outlook* (September 2013), Chapter 6, www.cbo.gov/publication/44521. The projected outcomes for debt incorporate the economic effects of the budget policies in the long run and the effects of that economic feedback on the budget. Those results are CBO's central estimates. They were derived from ranges determined on the basis of alternative assumptions about how much deficits "crowd out" investment in capital goods, such as factories and computers (because a larger portion of people's savings is being used to purchase government securities), and how much people respond to changes in after-tax wages by adjusting the number of hours they work.

Figure 4.

Federal Debt Held by the Public in CBO's Illustrative Scenarios With Smaller Deficits

(Percentage of gross domestic product)

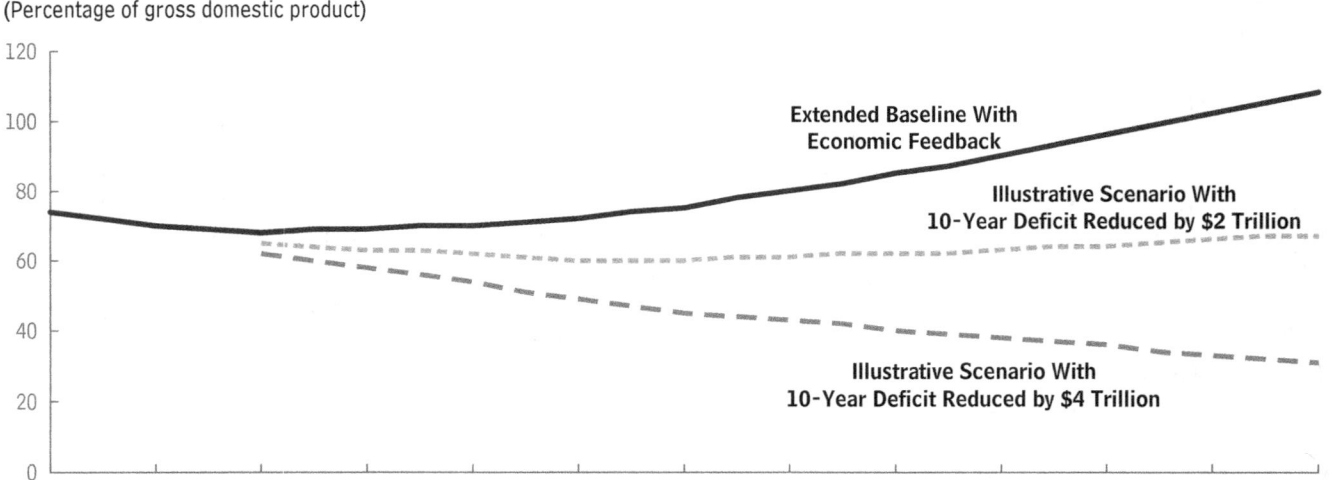

Source: Congressional Budget Office.

Notes: The extended baseline generally adheres closely to current law, following CBO's 10-year baseline budget projections through 2023 and then extending the baseline concept for the rest of the long-term projection period.

In the illustrative scenarios with the deficit reduced by $2 trillion and by $4 trillion between 2014 and 2023, those amounts are the cumulative reductions in deficits over that period, excluding interest savings, relative to the baseline. The reductions in the deficit as a percentage of output in 2023 are maintained in later years.

The results shown here do not include the economic effects of the scenarios from 2013 to 2017. Short-run economic effects are discussed in Congressional Budget Office, *The 2013 Long-Term Budget Outlook* (September 2013), Chapter 6, www.cbo.gov/publication/44521.

The results with economic feedback are CBO's central estimates from ranges determined on the basis of alternative assumptions about how much deficits "crowd out" investment in capital goods such as factories and computers (because a larger portion of people's savings is being used to purchase government securities) and how much people respond to changes in after-tax wages by adjusting the number of hours they work.

These data reflect recent revisions by the Bureau of Economic Analysis to estimates of gross domestic product (GDP) in past years and CBO's extrapolation of those revisions to projected future GDP.

possible policy changes come from a collection of budget options that CBO published in November 2013 in *Options for Reducing the Deficit: 2014 to 2023.* (That report also included a discussion of issues—not included here—that would be involved in eliminating a Cabinet department.)

The options presented in that report, and shown here in Tables 2 through 4, illustrate how challenging it would be to shrink deficits by as much as $2 trillion or $4 trillion over the 2014–2023 period. Very few policy changes that CBO has examined would be large enough, by themselves, to accomplish a sizable portion of that amount of deficit reduction.

To encourage the enactment of policy changes that would reduce deficits, some lawmakers and analysts have pro-

posed the adoption of "fiscal rules"—specific numerical targets for spending, revenues, deficits, or debt in future years—and of procedures that would take effect if those targets were not met.[17] According to the International Monetary Fund (IMF), few countries had fiscal rules until the 1990s, when the accumulation of debt led more governments to consider such rules to achieve fiscal sustainability.[18] By early 2012, 76 of the IMF's

17. For more information about fiscal rules, see Congressional Budget Office, *Choices for Deficit Reduction* (November 2012), "Appendix: Are Fiscal Rules a Useful Tool for Achieving Budgetary Goals?" www.cbo.gov/publication/43692.

18. See Andrea Schaechter and others, *Fiscal Rules in Response to the Crisis—Toward the "Next-Generation" Rules, a New Dataset,* Working Paper 12/187 (International Monetary Fund, July 2012), www.imf.org/external/pubs/cat/longres.aspx?sk=26094.0.

188 member countries had adopted either national rules, supranational rules, or both. Numerous other countries are actively considering such rules. The U.S. government has implemented fiscal rules and other constraints on budgetary decisions in the past and continues to employ them in the current budget process.

Merely adopting a fiscal rule, however, is not likely to improve budgetary outcomes.[19] In particular, experience in the United States and elsewhere suggests that fiscal rules are not a substitute for making difficult choices about the budget. Rather, they appear to be useful for enforcing budgetary goals mainly when consensus exists about those goals and about the policy changes needed to meet them because rules can make it harder for policymakers to succumb to pressure to stray from agreed-upon policy decisions.[20] But when consensus about budgetary goals erodes, rules will not necessarily stand in the way of policymakers who want to spend more or tax less than the rules allow.

Caveats About Options for Reducing the Deficit

The options included in this report are intended to reflect a range of possibilities rather than a ranking of priorities or a comprehensive list. Inclusion or exclusion of any particular option does not imply endorsement or disapproval

by CBO, and the report does not make recommendations. Many of the policy changes could be implemented in ways that would achieve more or less budgetary savings than are reported here. Moreover, numerous other policies that would decrease spending or increase revenues to a greater or lesser extent could be considered.

The estimates of the options' effects on the deficit over the 2014–2023 period are based on hypothetical proposals and are presented for illustrative purposes only. Estimates of legislative proposals related to these options might differ from the estimates shown here because of specific details contained in proposed legislation, because of revised baseline projections, or for other reasons.[21] Moreover, some of the options interact in ways that would cause their combined effect to differ from the sum of the individual effects described here.

The policy changes would differ in how their budgetary effects evolved over time. Options that were phased in gradually by, for example, applying only to people below a specific age would tend to have effects that grew more quickly over time than would options that were fully implemented right away. In addition, options that changed the annual growth rate of benefits would tend to have effects that grew more quickly over time (as the differences in growth rates compounded) than would options that changed the amount of benefits but not the rate of increase. Similarly, options that changed the way tax brackets are adjusted, or indexed, for inflation would have effects that grew more quickly over time than would options that immediately changed tax rates. Further, the more the deficit was reduced in earlier years, the greater the impact that reduction would have in lowering the government's future interest costs.

CBO's November 2013 volume of budget options summarizes some advantages and disadvantages of each of the options presented here. This report does not repeat those points, but a later section discusses broad criteria that

---

19. Researchers have tried to find a statistical relationship between fiscal rules and budget outcomes. A few studies have found a relationship between certain rules and improved fiscal performance (such as a given reduction in debt over a specified period). However, the studies noted that the results were not conclusive and could have been affected by other factors. For instance, a strong political commitment to fiscal discipline, which might be reflected in the introduction of a fiscal rule, could lead to improvements in budgetary performance that would have occurred even without the rule. See Kevin Fletcher and others, *United Kingdom: Selected Issues Paper,* Country Report 10/337 (International Monetary Fund, November 2010), www.imf.org/external/pubs/cat/longres.aspx?sk=24338.0; Manmohan Kumar and others, *Fiscal Rules—Anchoring Expectations for Sustainable Public Finances,* Policy Paper (International Monetary Fund, December 2009), www.imf.org/external/pp/longres.aspx?id=4402; and Stephanie Guichard and others, *What Promotes Fiscal Consolidation: OECD Country Experiences,* Economics Department Working Paper 553 (Organisation for Economic Co-operation and Development, May 2007), http://dx.doi.org/10.1787/180833424370.

20. See Allen Schick, "The Role of Fiscal Rules in Budgeting," *OECD Journal on Budgeting,* vol. 3, no. 3 (December 2003), pp. 7–34, www.oecd-ilibrary.org/governance/the-role-of-fiscal-rules-in-budgeting_budget-v3-art14-en.

21. For example, the recently passed Bipartisan Budget Act of 2013 reduces the potential budgetary effects of four options that CBO estimated in November 2013. Those options would change the terms and conditions for federal oil and gas leasing, increase federal insurance premiums for private pension plans, increase fees for aviation security, and increase federal civilian employees' contributions to their pensions. However, alternative versions of those options could be specified that would have larger or smaller effects than CBO estimated in November.

policymakers and the public might use when making choices about deficit reduction.

Options for Reducing Mandatory Spending

Mandatory spending—which totaled $2.0 trillion in 2013 or close to 60 percent of federal outlays—consists of all spending other than interest on federal debt that is not subject to annual appropriations. Lawmakers generally determine spending for mandatory programs by setting the programs' parameters, such as eligibility rules and benefit formulas, rather than by appropriating specific amounts each year. Mandatory spending is net of offsetting receipts—which consist of certain fees and other charges, such as premiums paid by beneficiaries.[22]

Nearly all mandatory outlays are for social insurance programs (in which most people who are eligible to participate do so and in which payments by participants represent at least part of the funding) or means-tested programs (which link eligibility to income). The largest mandatory programs are Social Security and Medicare. Those two programs alone accounted for 64 percent of mandatory outlays in 2013—or 38 percent of all federal spending. Medicaid and other health care programs accounted for another 14 percent of mandatory spending last year. The rest of mandatory spending is primarily for income security programs (such as unemployment compensation, nutrition assistance programs, and Supplemental Security Income), certain refundable tax credits, retirement benefits for civilian and military employees of the federal government, certain veterans' benefits, student loans, and agriculture programs.

The Context for Mandatory Spending Options. If no new laws were enacted that affected mandatory programs, CBO estimates, mandatory outlays would remain fairly stable as a share of the economy—between 12.6 percent and 13.1 percent of GDP from 2014 through 2021 but reaching 13.5 percent by 2023.[23] By comparison, such spending averaged 11.5 percent of GDP from 2003 to 2012 and 9.9 percent over the past four decades.

CBO's projections for total mandatory spending mask diverging trends for its different components. CBO projects that, under current law, spending for Social Security and the major health care programs, notably Medicare and Medicaid, would grow from 9.8 percent of GDP in 2014 to 11.2 percent by 2023, driven largely by the aging of the population, an expansion of federal subsidies for health insurance, and rising health care costs per person. At the same time, outlays for all other mandatory programs would decline relative to GDP, from 3.0 percent in 2014 to 2.3 percent by 2023. That projected decline reflects an anticipated continuation of the economic expansion, which would reduce the number of people who are eligible for many income security programs, and scheduled changes to tax provisions, which would reduce outlays arising from some tax credits.

The options discussed below are grouped into three broad categories: Social Security, health care programs, and other mandatory programs. They would generally decrease the amount paid to beneficiaries, redefine the population that is entitled to benefits of various programs, or reduce payments to state and local governments. Some options would create incentives for people to work longer or to save more before they retire, or have other economic and social consequences. (For 34 options encompassing a broad range of mandatory spending programs, see Table 2.)

Among the options related to health care programs, some would result in a reallocation of health care spending— from the federal government to businesses, households, or state governments—and most would give parties other than the federal government stronger incentives to control costs while exposing them to more financial risk. In addition to their effects on the federal budget, therefore, the options would have a variety of other consequences: For example, some are designed to affect people's behavior as they obtain services in the health care system, and some focus on influencing the actions of health care providers, health insurers, or state governments. As a result, a number of the options would shift the sources or types of health insurance coverage that people obtain or cause people to seek and providers to deliver different types of health care. Whether the options would lead health care

---

22. Unlike revenues, which are collected through the exercise of the government's sovereign powers (for example, by levying income taxes), offsetting receipts are generally collected from other government accounts or from members of the public through businesslike transactions. They include, for example, Medicare premiums and rental payments and royalties for the extraction of oil or gas from public lands. In this report, spending for Medicare is reported net of offsetting receipts.

23. For a more detailed discussion of the components of mandatory spending and CBO's baseline budget projections, see Congressional Budget Office, *Updated Budget Projections: Fiscal Years 2013–2023* (May 2013), www.cbo.gov/publication/44172.

Table 2.

Savings From Options to Reduce Mandatory Spending, 2014 to 2023

Option	Estimated Savings (Billions of dollars)
Social Security	
Reduce Social Security Benefits for New Beneficiaries by 15 Percent	188
Link Initial Social Security Benefits to Average Prices Instead of Average Earnings	58 to 93
Raise the Full Retirement Age for Social Security	58
Lengthen by Three Years the Computation Period for Social Security Benefits	43
Require Social Security Disability Insurance Applicants to Have Worked More in Recent Years	35
Eliminate Eligibility for Starting Social Security Disability Benefits at Age 62 or Later	11
Health Care Programs	
Impose Caps on Federal Spending for Medicaid	105 to 606
Increase Premiums for Parts B and D of Medicare	287
Convert Medicare to a Premium Support System	22 to 275
Add a "Public Plan" to the Health Insurance Exchanges	158
Require Manufacturers to Pay a Minimum Rebate on Drugs Covered Under Part D of Medicare for Low-Income Beneficiaries	123
Change the Cost-Sharing Rules for Medicare and Restrict Medigap Insurance	114
Eliminate Exchange Subsidies for People With Income Over 300 Percent of the Federal Poverty Guidelines	109
Limit Medical Malpractice Torts	64[a]
Bundle Medicare's Payments to Health Care Providers	17 to 47
Introduce Minimum Out-of-Pocket Requirements Under TRICARE for Life	31
Raise the Age of Eligibility for Medicare to 67	19
Other Programs	
Convert Multiple Assistance Programs for Lower-Income People Into Smaller Block Grants to States	404[a]
Use an Alternative Measure of Inflation to Index Social Security and Other Mandatory Programs	162
Eliminate Concurrent Receipt of Retirement Pay and Disability Compensation for Disabled Veterans	108
Eliminate Supplemental Security Income Benefits for Children	103[a]
Eliminate the Add-On to Pell Grants That Is Funded With Mandatory Spending	76
Tighten Eligibility and Determinations of Income for the Supplemental Nutrition Assistance Program	50
Reduce or Eliminate Subsidized Loans for Undergraduate Students	18 to 41
Reduce Subsidies in the Crop Insurance Program	27
Eliminate Direct Payments to Agricultural Producers	25
Narrow Eligibility for Veterans' Disability Compensation by Excluding Certain Disabilities Unrelated to Military Duties	20
Reduce Subsidies to Fannie Mae and Freddie Mac	19
Restrict VA's Individual Unemployability Benefits to Disabled Veterans Who Are Younger Than the Full Retirement Age for Social Security	15
Limit Enrollment in Department of Agriculture Conservation Programs	13
Eliminate Subsidies for Certain Meals in the National School Lunch and School Breakfast Programs	10
Change the Terms and Conditions for Federal Oil and Gas Leasing	6
Reduce the Amounts of Federal Pensions	6
Increase Federal Insurance Premiums for Private Pension Plans	5

Source: Congressional Budget Office, *Options for Reducing the Deficit: 2014 to 2023* (November 2013), www.cbo.gov/publication/44715.

Notes: In cases where the option would also affect revenues, the savings shown include effects on both mandatory spending and revenues.

　　　VA = Department of Veterans Affairs.

a. This option would also affect discretionary spending; that effect is not included in this amount.

to be delivered more efficiently, to be applied more appropriately, or to be of higher quality than it would otherwise be would hinge on the responses of those affected.

Adopting just a few of the options with the largest savings would not, by itself, achieve either of the possible goals for deficit reduction mentioned above. For example, if lawmakers wanted to reduce deficits by $2 trillion (excluding interest savings) over the coming decade, the federal budgetary savings from enacting three of the largest options in Table 2 would achieve about 60 percent of that goal.[24] Those three options would reduce Social Security benefits by 15 percent, limit federal spending on Medicaid by capping the amount that each state receives from the federal government to operate the program, and convert multiple assistance programs to block grants. If the goal was to reduce deficits by $4 trillion, that set of changes would achieve only 30 percent of the goal.

Those three options would have quite different effects on spending relative to the sizes of the programs involved. For example, between 2015 and 2023, those three options would reduce total spending on Social Security by 2 percent but total spending on one of the assistance programs—the Supplemental Nutrition Assistance Program, or SNAP—by about 40 percent.

Many of the policy changes listed here could be implemented in ways that would produce greater budgetary savings, but such alternatives would generally impose larger burdens on program beneficiaries, state governments, or health care providers than the versions shown here. Some of the options would save significantly more in later years than in the first decade.

Options for Social Security. Under current law, spending for Social Security would total more than $11 trillion over the next decade, CBO estimates. The largest savings among the options included here—$188 billion—would stem from reducing initial Social Security benefits by 15 percent. Another option—using an alternative measure for inflation when computing cost-of-living adjustments for benefits—would save $108 billion in outlays for Social Security over the 2014–2023 period (and $54 billion in outlays for other programs). Other

options listed in the table would produce somewhat smaller savings over the next 10 years. However, many of the options shown for changing Social Security would save substantially more in subsequent years than in the first 10 years, including raising the full retirement age and linking initial benefits to average prices instead of average earnings.

Options for Health Care Programs. The federal government's mandatory health care programs include Medicare, Medicaid, CHIP, subsidies provided through new health insurance exchanges and related spending, the Federal Employees Health Benefits program for civilian retirees, and the TRICARE for Life program for military retirees. Under current law, total spending for those programs would total about $12.3 trillion over the coming decade, CBO estimates.

For each of the options included here that would affect spending for health care programs, the amount of federal savings and the consequences for stakeholders—beneficiaries, employers, health care providers, insurers, and states—would depend crucially on the specific details of any legislation designed to achieve them. For example, the option to limit federal spending on Medicaid would cap the amount that each state receives from the federal government to operate the program; depending on the specifications of the cap, the federal government's savings could range from $105 billion to $606 billion over the next decade, CBO estimates.

Six of the options included here would make changes to the Medicare program. Three of the options would affect the share of Medicare costs that beneficiaries pay and could be designed to affect people's behavior as they obtain Medicare coverage or services in the health care system. These options would increase premiums for Medicare, convert Medicare to a premium support system, and change the cost-sharing rules for Medicare and restrict medigap insurance. Two other options—bundling Medicare's payments to health care providers and requiring manufacturers to pay rebates for drugs provided to low-income beneficiaries—focus on providers of health care services and supplies. Finally, one option would reduce the number of people receiving benefits by raising the age at which people become eligible for Medicare. Savings for the options affecting Medicare included here would range from $19 billion to $287 billion over the next 10 years.

---

24. That figure is based on the alternative under the option to impose caps on federal spending for Medicaid that would result in the largest savings.

Two of the options listed here would alter the expansion of health care coverage under the ACA. They would eliminate exchange subsidies for people with income above 300 percent of the federal poverty guidelines or add a "public plan" to the health insurance exchanges; each would save more than $100 billion over 10 years. Another, much broader approach related to the ACA would be to repeal the provisions of the act that expand Medicaid coverage and provide subsidies for health insurance purchased through exchanges, along with other related changes in law. That option is not listed in the table (because it was not addressed in detail in *Options for Reducing the Deficit: 2014 to 2023*), but the budgetary savings from repealing those coverage provisions would be close to their net costs under current law, which CBO and JCT estimated most recently to be about $1.4 trillion over the 2014–2023 period. In addition to the budgetary effects, the repeal of those provisions would greatly increase the number of people who would be uninsured over the next decade compared with the number under current law, and would have many other effects as well. Repeal of the entire law, which includes provisions that will reduce other spending and boost revenues, would, on net, increase budget deficits, CBO and JCT estimate.

Options for Mandatory Programs Other Than Social Security and Health Care. Mandatory programs other than Social Security and health care programs account for a much smaller share of federal spending; under current law, expenditures on those programs would total about $5.3 trillion over the next decade, CBO estimates. Consequently, the options for changing them would generally produce smaller savings except in those cases in which the changes represented very large cuts to funding for those programs in percentage terms. For example, one option included here would convert several assistance programs for lower-income people into smaller block grants (shown in the third panel of Table 2). The option would generate more than $400 billion in savings through 2023 but would result in large cuts to those programs—for example, spending for child nutrition programs would be reduced by one-third from the amount that is projected to be spent under current law.

Options included here that involve education programs—reducing the maximum grant available in the Pell grant program (by eliminating mandatory funding) or reducing or eliminating subsidized loans for undergraduate students—would save between $18 billion and $76 billion in mandatory spending through 2023. CBO

has also analyzed a number of changes to smaller mandatory programs. For example, a set of changes to agriculture programs—limiting enrollment in the Department of Agriculture's conservation programs, reducing subsidies in the crop insurance program, and eliminating direct payments to agricultural producers for certain commodities—would save a total of roughly $65 billion over the decade.

Options for Reducing Discretionary Spending

Discretionary spending—the portion of federal spending that lawmakers control through annual appropriation acts—totaled about $1.2 trillion in 2013 or about 35 percent of federal outlays. Those discretionary outlays pay for a wide variety of federal activities, including most programs related to national defense, transportation, elementary and secondary education, veterans' health care, international affairs, and law enforcement. Because lawmakers set funding for discretionary programs each year, cutting spending through the regular appropriation process can ensure only short-term savings. To mandate longer-term savings, lawmakers could continue using an approach that has been used at times in the past and is being used today—that is, setting limits on the amount of appropriations that can be provided in future years.

Since the 1970s, the share of federal spending that occurs through the annual appropriation process has dropped considerably. Specifically, between 1973 and 2013, discretionary spending fell from 53 percent of total federal spending to about 35 percent. Relative to the size of the economy, discretionary spending declined from 9.6 percent of GDP in 1973 to a low of 6.0 percent in 1999 before rising back to 7.2 percent in 2013. Most of the decline over that period involved spending for national defense, which, as a share of GDP, reached a low of 2.9 percent around 2000. However, such outlays began climbing again relative to GDP shortly thereafter, reaching an average of 4.6 percent from 2009 through 2011. Roughly half of the growth in defense spending over the 2001–2011 period resulted from spending on operations in Iraq and Afghanistan. In 2013, discretionary spending for defense fell to 3.8 percent of GDP.

Nondefense discretionary spending has generally ranged from about 3 percent to 4 percent of GDP over the past four decades. One exception was from 1975 to 1981, when such spending averaged almost 5 percent of GDP. Another exception was from 2009 through 2011, when funding from the American Recovery and Reinvestment

Act of 2009 and from other sources associated with the federal government's response to the 2007–2009 recession helped push nondefense discretionary outlays above 4 percent of GDP. Like defense discretionary spending, nondefense discretionary outlays as a share of GDP fell in 2013, to 3.5 percent.

Under current law, most discretionary appropriations through 2021 are constrained by the caps put in place by the Budget Control Act of 2011 (as modified by subsequent legislation).[25] Assuming that future legislation adheres to the current caps (including the automatic reductions in those caps required by the act) and that discretionary appropriations grow at the rate of inflation after 2021 (the assumptions that underlie CBO's baseline projections), outlays from those appropriations are projected to decline from 7.2 percent of GDP in 2013— already below the 40-year average of 8.4 percent—to 5.3 percent in 2023. That amount would be the lowest level of discretionary spending relative to GDP in more than half a century (since at least 1962, the first year for which comparable data are available). Under those projections, defense and nondefense discretionary spending would each equal 2.6 percent of GDP in 2023, which would also be the smallest share of the economy for each category in at least five decades.

Current Caps on Discretionary Funding and Their Relationship to Possible Deficit Reduction Goals. In dollar terms, discretionary outlays are projected to total $12.8 trillion over the 2014–2023 period, split roughly equally between defense and nondefense spending. If policymakers wanted to reduce deficits by $2 trillion (excluding interest savings) over the next decade entirely through cuts in discretionary spending, they would need to cut such spending by more than 15 percent relative to those projections; to reduce deficits by $4 trillion, policymakers would need to cut such spending by more than 30 percent.

To achieve deficit reduction through changes in discretionary spending, lawmakers would need to reduce the

---

25. The statutory caps do not constrain funding for overseas contingency operations (such as military operations in Afghanistan), emergencies, disaster relief, and certain program integrity initiatives (which identify and reduce overpayments in some benefit programs); the caps will be adjusted to accommodate funding for those purposes.

statutory funding caps below the levels established under current law or enact appropriations below those caps. The discretionary spending options included here could be used to accomplish either of those objectives (see Table 3).

Alternatively, some of the options could be implemented to comply with the existing caps on discretionary funding rather than to reduce deficits further. For example, as discussed in more detail below, savings from some of the defense options might bridge part of the gap between the costs of the Department of Defense's (DoD's) plans and the existing caps. (The savings shown for most of the defense options are measured relative to DoD's plans rather than CBO's baseline projections.) The savings from specific reductions in appropriations like those presented here also could be used to create room for an increase in appropriations for other, higher-priority purposes—while keeping total discretionary appropriations at or very close to the current statutory caps.

Overall, because of the caps established under the Budget Control Act, discretionary outlays are projected to be $1.4 trillion lower over the 2014–2023 period than they would be if the funding provided for 2013 was continued in later years with increases for inflation; that difference would mean that, during the decade as a whole, real annual outlays for a large collection of government programs and activities would be 11 percent below the amount in 2013. The reduction in discretionary outlays that would be accomplished by implementing all of the options presented here other than those involving military force structure or acquisition (which CBO measured relative to DoD's plans rather than to its baseline) would account for a little more than 55 percent of that $1.4 trillion difference.

Options for Reducing Defense Spending. Under the current caps, funding for defense will be well below the amounts that would be needed to implement DoD's plans. Specifically, outlays for defense over the next decade under those caps are projected to be about $750 billion below what they would be if the funding appropriated for 2013 was continued in later years with increases for inflation. For DoD, which accounts for about 95 percent of the federal resources devoted to defense, outlays under the caps over the next 10 years are projected to be about $600 billion below the amounts

Table 3.

Savings From Options to Reduce Discretionary Spending, 2014 to 2023

Option	Estimated Savings (Billions of dollars)
Defense	
Reduce the Size of the Military to Satisfy Caps Under the Budget Control Act	495[a]
Modify TRICARE Enrollment Fees and Cost Sharing for Working-Age Military Retirees	20 to 71[b]
Replace the Joint Strike Fighter Program With F-16s and F/A-18s	37[a]
Cap Increases in Basic Pay for Military Service Members	25
Defer Development of a New Long-Range Bomber	24[a]
Replace Some Military Personnel With Civilian Employees	19
Cancel the Littoral Combat Ship Program	12[a]
Cancel the Army's Ground Combat Vehicle Program	11[a]
Reduce the Number of Ballistic Missile Submarines	11[a]
Stop Building Ford Class Aircraft Carriers	10[a]
Nondefense	
Reduce Funding for International Affairs Programs	114
Eliminate Human Space Exploration Programs	73
Restrict Pell Grants to the Neediest Students	1 to 68[b]
Limit Highway Funding to Expected Highway Revenues	65
Eliminate or Reduce Funding for Certain Grants to State and Local Governments	55
Reduce the Annual Across-the-Board Adjustment for Federal Civilian Employees' Pay	53
End Enrollment in VA Medical Care for Veterans in Priority Groups 7 and 8	48[b]
Reduce the Size of the Federal Workforce Through Attrition	43
Reduce or Constrain Funding for the National Institutes of Health	13 to 28
Increase Payments by Tenants in Federally Assisted Housing	22
Impose Fees to Cover the Cost of Government Regulations and Charge for Services Provided to the Private Sector	21
Eliminate Subsidies for Amtrak	15
Eliminate Capital Investment Grants for Transit Systems	14
Repeal the Davis-Bacon Act	13
Increase Fees for Aviation Security	11
Eliminate Federal Funding for National Community Service and Senior Community Service Employment Programs	11
Reduce Department of Energy Funding for Energy Technology Development	9
Eliminate Grants to Large and Medium-Sized Airports	8
Eliminate Certain Forest Service Programs	5
Reduce Federal Funding for the Arts and Humanities	5
Eliminate the International Trade Administration's Trade Promotion Activities	3

Source: Congressional Budget Office, *Options for Reducing the Deficit: 2014 to 2023* (November 2013), www.cbo.gov/publication/44715.

Notes: The savings shown are the decrease in discretionary outlays. For most discretionary spending options, the decrease in outlays is presented relative to CBO's baseline projections for individual components of discretionary spending, which incorporate the assumption that current appropriations continue in later years with adjustments for projected inflation. In total, the funding projected in the inflation-adjusted amounts is greater than the caps on discretionary funding. Some of the discretionary options related to defense are measured relative to the Department of Defense's (DoD's) estimates of the costs for its plans rather than CBO's baseline projections. The costs of DoD's plans are greater than the caps on defense funding. To reduce deficits through changes in discretionary spending, lawmakers would need to reduce the statutory funding caps below the levels already established under current law or enact appropriations below those caps; the options shown could be used to accomplish either of those objectives.

VA = Department of Veterans Affairs.

a.   Savings are based on the fiscal year 2014 Future Years Defense Program and CBO's extension of that program.

b.   This option would also affect mandatory spending and, in the case of TRICARE, revenues as well. Those effects are not included in this amount.

in DoD's plans (as detailed in its 2014 Future Years Defense Program, or FYDP, and other long-term planning documents).[26]

If policymakers wanted to reduce defense spending, they could reduce the number of major combat units that the military services field (Army brigade combat teams, Navy combatant ships, Air Force fighter squadrons, and so forth), reduce funding for acquiring equipment and for operations, or adopt some combination of those two approaches, with the following broad implications:[27]

■ *Reducing the number of military units fielded* would leave the units that remained in the force funded at levels that have produced today's highly capable forces. However, having fewer such forces might jeopardize the military's capacity to respond to multiple conflicts simultaneously or to engage in prolonged conflicts without requiring long overseas deployments for service members.

■ *Reducing the average funding per unit for equipping and operating military units* would maintain the size of the force at planned levels. However, lower funding per unit would result in some combination of fewer

---

26. In comparing the costs of DoD's plans with those under the statutory caps, CBO assumed that DoD would receive 95.5 percent of the funding limit for defense (which equals DoD's average share of that funding in base budgets from 2002 to 2011). DoD's 2014 FYDP includes the department's intended funding requests for the 2014–2018 period, which are based on the Administration's plans for military and civilian personnel levels, procurement and maintenance of weapon systems, and operational intensity. Through 2018, the budgetary effects of the options shown here that involve force structure or acquisition are based on DoD's estimates of the costs of its plans. From 2019 through 2023, those budgetary effects are based on an extension of the FYDP that uses DoD's estimates if such estimates are available (for example, the Navy prepares an annual 30-year shipbuilding plan) and on CBO's projections of price and compensation trends for the overall economy if they are not. Although the budgetary effects of the options are estimated on the basis of DoD's estimated costs, CBO anticipates that many elements of DoD's plans would cost more than the amounts budgeted in the department's FYDP and CBO's extension of the FYDP. For more about those higher costs, see Congressional Budget Office, *Long-Term Implications of the 2014 Future Years Defense Program* (November 2013), www.cbo.gov/publication/44683.

27. For more information, see Congressional Budget Office, *Approaches for Scaling Back the Defense Department's Budget Plans* (March 2013), www.cbo.gov/publication/43997.

or delayed purchases of new weapons, decreased peacetime operations, and less training, which might affect the military's superiority relative to the forces of other countries.

For the most part, the budgetary effects of discretionary spending options were calculated relative to CBO's baseline projections. But because the baseline projections do not reflect programmatic details for force structure and specific weapon systems, the effects of options involving those aspects of the defense budget (the 1st, 3rd, 5th, and 7th through 10th options listed in Table 3) are calculated relative to DoD's 2014 FYDP. Because DoD's estimates of the costs of implementing the FYDP exceed CBO's baseline projections for defense spending, the options involving military force structure and acquisition are not necessarily ways to reduce the deficits projected in CBO's baseline; at least in part, those options represent ways to reduce DoD's planned spending so that it more closely aligns with the amounts projected in the baseline.

For example, CBO examined one large, comprehensive option that would entail reducing the size of the military by cutting planned numbers of soldiers, planes, and ships. That option would result in savings relative to DoD's plans of close to $500 billion over the next decade and would bring defense spending in 2017 close to the limits imposed by the Budget Control Act. Other options that would target specific programs, such as halting construction of new aircraft carriers, reducing the number of ballistic missile submarines, or replacing the Joint Strike Fighter Program with the most advanced versions of fighter aircraft already in production (F-16s and F/A-18s), would result in savings of between $10 billion and $37 billion over the 2014–2023 period. Possible changes to the military health care program, TRICARE, that are listed here could reduce discretionary spending by as much as $71 billion over 10 years (with some effects on other components of the budget). Enacting all of the options included here, apart from the comprehensive one just discussed, would reduce spending by a far smaller amount than would be necessary to comply with the caps under current law.

Options for Reducing Nondefense Spending. Cuts in nondefense discretionary spending could affect a broad range of activities, including programs related to transportation, education, international affairs, veterans' health care, and law enforcement. About half of nondefense discretionary spending in 2012 (the most recent year for which information is available), or $307 billion, could be regarded as investment—that is, spending that is expected to provide benefits for some years in the future.[28] The federal government invests in physical capital by funding the construction of infrastructure, such as highways and government facilities, and by purchasing equipment, such as computers. In addition, the federal government supports research and development that occurs in government laboratories, at universities, and in the private sector, and it invests in education and in job and vocational training to promote a skilled and productive workforce.

The current caps on nondefense spending will require agencies to operate with significantly fewer real resources in future years than they received last year. Specifically, under the caps, such spending is projected to be about $650 billion lower during the next decade than if funding for 2013 was continued with adjustments for inflation. In some cases, even if funding was continued with inflation adjustments, the resources would be insufficient to maintain the services currently provided; for example, the costs of health care for veterans tend to grow faster than the rate of inflation. Therefore, complying with the funding limits under the Budget Control Act would require substantial cuts in the scope of nondefense discretionary programs, and cutting deficits below the amounts projected in CBO's baseline (which incorporates those caps) through reductions in nondefense discretionary spending would require even larger cuts in those programs.

As shown in Table 3, CBO examined several options for changing nondefense discretionary programs that would produce sizable savings—from tens of billions of dollars to $114 billion over the next decade—including the following: significantly reducing funding for international affairs programs, eliminating NASA's human spaceflight programs, restricting Pell grants to the neediest students, and limiting the amount of highway funding to match the highway revenues expected to be collected at current tax rates. Other options would produce smaller savings, in part because the amounts of funding provided for most individual discretionary programs are relatively small. Compared with what spending would be if 2013 appropriations were continued with adjustments for inflation, enacting all of the nondefense options shown here would reduce spending by as much as $685 billion over the

2014–2023 period—just a little more than is needed to meet the caps.

In addition to their effects on the federal budget, the options would have a variety of other consequences. For example, many federal programs (including some of those geared toward federal investment) provide funds to state and local governments; those funds accounted for about a third of nondefense discretionary spending in 2012. Reducing federal support for such programs would force other levels of government to make decisions about decreasing the scope of the programs, increasing their own funding, or some combination of the two.

Options for Increasing Revenues

In 2013, the federal government collected $2.8 trillion in revenues. Individual income taxes were the largest source of revenues, accounting for 47 percent of the total. Social insurance taxes (primarily payroll taxes collected to support Social Security and Medicare) accounted for 34 percent; about 10 percent came from corporate income taxes; and other receipts (from excise taxes, estate and gift taxes, earnings of the Federal Reserve System, customs duties, and miscellaneous fees and fines) made up the remaining 9 percent.

Over the past 40 years, total federal revenues have averaged 17.4 percent of GDP—ranging from a high of 19.9 percent of GDP in 2000 to a low of 14.6 percent in 2009 and 2010. The variation over time in total revenues as a percentage of GDP is primarily the result of fluctuations in receipts of individual income tax payments and, to a lesser extent, of fluctuations in collections of corporate income taxes. In 2013, revenues equaled 16.7 percent of GDP.

Looking ahead, revenues are projected to increase under current law to 17.7 percent of GDP in 2014 and to 18.6 percent in 2015, and then to remain between 18 percent and 19 percent of GDP from 2016 through 2023. About half of the expected increase in the next two years stems from scheduled changes in tax rules, such as the expiration at the end of December 2013 of enhanced depreciation deductions allowed for certain business investments. Accounting for the other half are factors related mainly to the strengthening economy, including increases relative to GDP in some components of taxable income (such as wages and salaries, capital gains realizations, proprietors' income, and domestic economic profits) and the continued rise to more normal levels of the ratio of corporate income taxes to domestic economic

---

28. For more information, see Congressional Budget Office, *Federal Investment* (December 2013), www.cbo.gov/publication/44974.

profits. Under current law, between 2015 and 2023, individual income tax receipts are projected to rise relative to GDP, as increases in taxpayers' real income push more income into higher tax brackets, but corporate income tax receipts and remittances to the Treasury from the Federal Reserve are projected to fall relative to GDP.

Lawmakers could raise revenues further by modifying existing taxes—either by increasing tax rates or by expanding tax bases (the measures, such as personal or corporate income, on which taxes are assessed)—or by imposing new taxes on income, consumption, or particular activities. All of those approaches would have effects not only on the amount of revenues collected, but also on economic activity, the distribution of the tax burden among households, and the complexity of the tax system.

CBO's November 2013 volume of budget options contains a wide variety of alternatives for raising revenues (shown in Table 4). Those options, which were analyzed by CBO and JCT, include changes to income tax rates and the income tax bases for individuals and corporations, expansions of payroll taxes, increases in excise taxes, and several new taxes.[29] Although CBO's report included fewer options for increasing revenues than for cutting spending, many of the potential changes to revenues would have larger effects on the deficit than the potential changes to individual spending programs.

Raising Tax Rates. Because revenues from individual income taxes and payroll taxes constitute over 80 percent of total federal revenues, increasing the rates of those taxes by just 1 percentage point would result in a sizable reduction in the deficit. For example, boosting all individual income tax rates on ordinary income (all income subject to the income tax except long-term capital gains and certain dividends) by 1 percentage point would increase revenues by $694 billion over 10 years, according to JCT's estimates. And a 1 percentage-point increase in the combined payroll tax rate paid by employees and employers for Medicare hospital insurance would raise $859 billion over the 2014–2023 period, JCT estimates, or over 40 percent of the savings required to meet a goal of reducing the deficit by $2 trillion.

However, those increases in revenues would be much smaller if rate increases were applied to a narrower tax base. For example, boosting rates on ordinary income in the top four brackets—those with statutory tax rates of 28 percent or more—by 1 percentage point would raise revenues by $152 billion from 2014 through 2023, according to JCT. Raising corporate income tax rates would produce smaller but still significant amounts of revenues: JCT projects that a 1 percentage-point increase in those rates would yield an estimated $113 billion over 10 years.

Broadening Tax Bases. In combination, three of the largest tax expenditures in the individual income tax—itemized deductions for state and local taxes, home mortgage interest, and charitable contributions—equal nearly 1 percent of GDP. Thus, eliminating or substantially reducing those deductions would cause revenues to increase by a substantial amount. For example, repealing the deduction for state and local taxes would, according to JCT, raise $954 billion from 2014 through 2023—just about half of the way toward a possible $2 trillion goal for deficit reduction. As another example, limiting the deduction for charitable contributions to donations in excess of 2 percent of adjusted gross income would increase revenues by $212 billion over the 10-year period, JCT estimates.[30]

Alternatively, the income and payroll tax bases could be expanded through the inclusion of more sources of income. For example, the federal tax code gives preferential treatment to payments for health insurance and health care, primarily through the exclusion from income and payroll taxes of most premium payments for employment-based health insurance and other employment-based contributions for health care. CBO and JCT estimate that limiting those exclusions to $6,420 for individual coverage and $15,620 for family coverage beginning in January 2015 (with both amounts subsequently indexed for inflation) and simultaneously eliminating the new excise tax on employment-based health benefits scheduled to begin in 2018 would reduce the deficit by $537 billion over the ten-year period. Increasing the taxable portion of Social Security and Railroad Retirement benefits so that those benefits are taxed in the same way as distributions from defined benefit pension plans would raise $388 billion from 2014 through 2023, JCT estimates. And increasing the

---

29. The options shown in the table are illustrative. They could be combined as part of a comprehensive deficit reduction plan, but the total additional revenues from such a combination would probably differ from the sum of the revenues shown for the individual options because of interactions among the provisions.

---

30. Adjusted gross income includes income from all sources not specifically excluded by the tax code, minus certain deductions.

Table 4.

Deficit Reduction From Options to Increase Revenues, 2014 to 2023

Option	Estimated Deficit Reduction (Billions of dollars)
Individual Income Tax	
Eliminate the Deduction for State and Local Taxes	954
Increase Individual Income Tax Rates	98 to 694
Tax Social Security and Railroad Retirement Benefits in the Same Way That Distributions From Defined Benefit Pensions Are Taxed	388
Include Employer-Paid Premiums for Income Replacement Insurance in Employees' Taxable Income	326
Curtail the Deduction for Charitable Giving	212
Include Investment Income From Life Insurance and Annuities in Taxable Income	210
Eliminate Certain Tax Preferences for Education Expenses	155
Limit the Value of Itemized Deductions	71 to 146
Use an Alternative Measure of Inflation to Index Some Parameters of the Tax Code	140
Include All Income That U.S. Citizens Earn Abroad in Taxable Income	89
Further Limit Annual Contributions to Retirement Plans	89
Implement a New Minimum Tax on Adjusted Gross Income	76
Raise the Tax Rates on Long-Term Capital Gains and Dividends by 2 Percentage Points	53
Convert the Mortgage Interest Deduction to a 15 Percent Tax Credit	52
Eliminate the Tax Exemption for New Qualified Private Activity Bonds	31
Tax Carried Interest as Ordinary Income	17
Lower the Investment Income Limit for the Earned Income Tax Credit and Extend That Limit to the Refundable Portion of the Child Tax Credit	11
Other Revenues	
Impose a Tax on Emissions of Greenhouse Gases	1,060
Increase the Payroll Tax Rate for Medicare Hospital Insurance by 1 Percentage Point	859
Reduce Tax Preferences for Employment-Based Health Insurance	240 to 537
Increase the Maximum Taxable Earnings for the Social Security Payroll Tax	460
Increase Excise Taxes on Motor Fuels by 35 Cents and Index for Inflation	452
Extend the Period for Depreciating the Cost of Certain Investments	272
Repeal the Deduction for Domestic Production Activities	192
Impose a Tax on Financial Transactions	180
Tax All Pass-Through Business Owners Under SECA and Impose a Material Participation Standard	129
Increase Corporate Income Tax Rates by 1 Percentage Point	113
Repeal the "LIFO" and "Lower of Cost or Market" Inventory Accounting Methods	112
Expand Social Security Coverage to Include Newly Hired State and Local Government Employees	81
Increase All Taxes on Alcoholic Beverages to $16 per Proof Gallon	64
Impose a Fee on Large Financial Institutions	64
Determine Foreign Tax Credits on a Pooling Basis	44
Repeal the Low-Income Housing Tax Credit	41
Increase the Excise Tax on Cigarettes by 50 Cents per Pack	37
Repeal Certain Tax Preferences for Extractive Industries	34
Increase Federal Civilian Employees' Contributions to Their Pensions	19
Increase Taxes That Finance the Federal Share of the Unemployment Insurance System	14 to 15
Modify the Rules for the Sourcing of Income From Exports	6

Source: Congressional Budget Office, *Options for Reducing the Deficit: 2014 to 2023* (November 2013), www.cbo.gov/publication/44715.

Notes: In cases where the option would also affect mandatory spending, the deficit reduction shown includes effects on both revenues and mandatory spending.

SECA = Self-Employment Contributions Act; LIFO = last in, first out.

maximum amount of earnings subject to the Social Security tax—from 83 percent of earnings (in 2011) to 90 percent of earnings—would reduce the deficit by $460 billion over the 10-year period, according to JCT.

Imposing a New Tax. The option in Table 4 with the largest revenue effect would create a new source of revenues by imposing a tax on most emissions of greenhouse gases in the United States. Set at $25 per metric ton, such a tax would, according to JCT, raise over a trillion dollars—half of the savings necessary to meet a $2 trillion goal of deficit reduction over the next decade and a quarter of what would be needed for $4 trillion in deficit reduction.

Other new taxes could be narrower, such as imposing a tax on the purchase of most stocks and bonds and on transactions involving derivatives (contracts that derive their value from another security or commodity). JCT estimates that a financial transactions tax—set at 0.01 percent of the value of the security or, in the case of derivative contracts, at 0.01 percent of all payments to be made under the terms of the contract—would increase revenues by $180 billion from 2014 through 2023.

Other Approaches to Raising Revenues. Several comprehensive approaches to increasing revenues—each with the potential to increase them substantially—have received some attention lately (see Box 1). One approach would eliminate or reduce the value of all or most tax expenditures. Another strategy would create a value-added tax (VAT) on consumption. Closing the tax gap—the amount of revenues forgone each year because of noncompliance with the tax code—would be another potential source of revenues.

However, the change in revenues that would arise from implementing those broad proposals is uncertain. One reason for that uncertainty is that proposals for such comprehensive changes to the tax code are often combined with proposals to lower individual and corporate income tax rates or (in the case of some proposals to create a VAT) to replace an existing tax. Another reason for that uncertainty is that the effects of such broad policy changes would depend greatly on their specifications.

What Criteria Might Be Used to Evaluate Policy Changes?

Reducing federal budget deficits substantially relative to those projected under current law would require significant changes in policies governing federal spending,

federal revenues, or both. The rest of this report discusses four criteria that policymakers and the public might consider when evaluating budget plans:

■ What role would the federal government play in society?

■ How much would deficits be reduced in the next few years, the next 10 years, and subsequent decades?

■ What would be the economic impact in the short term and the long term?

■ Who would bear the burden of proposed changes in tax and spending policies?

The way that people think about those criteria, and the relative importance they attach to such considerations, will vary according to their individual preferences and priorities.

What Role Would the Federal Government Play in Society?

In considering policies aimed at reducing deficits, policymakers and the public would need to make judgments about the proper size and scope of the federal government, including the types of activities they consider appropriate for the government to carry out or subsidize and the weight they give to various types of spending and to various benefits conveyed through the tax system.

If lawmakers opted, for example, to maintain revenues at the levels projected under current law (an estimated 18.3 percent of GDP over the coming decade), they would need to cut noninterest spending by 5 percent to achieve a $2 billion reduction in deficits (excluding interest savings) over the decade; a $4 billion reduction in deficits would require a 10 percent cut in noninterest spending. If lawmakers opted to set revenues at about 17½ percent of GDP (close to the average percentage over the past 40 years), spending cuts would have to be larger.

Alternatively, lawmakers could opt to maintain noninterest spending at the levels projected under current law (an estimated 18.8 percent of GDP over the coming decade), in which case such reductions in deficits would require increases in revenues of roughly 5 percent or 10 percent, respectively. Those approaches would result in higher taxes relative to the size of the economy than the nation has been accustomed to paying. If lawmakers

Box 1.

Some Approaches for Raising Revenues Not Included in *Options for Reducing the Deficit: 2014 to 2023*

Some comprehensive changes to the tax system—such as eliminating all or most tax expenditures, implementing a value-added tax (VAT), or closing the tax gap—could potentially reduce the deficit by hundreds of billions of dollars or more over the next decade, or they could be part of a broader, revenue-neutral package of changes that would improve economic efficiency and thereby boost overall output and income. However, other considerations might constrain the amount of additional revenue that would result from adopting one of those approaches.

Eliminating or Limiting Most or All Tax Expenditures

Certain provisions in the tax code—including exclusions, deductions, exemptions, preferential tax rates, and credits—are called tax expenditures because they resemble government spending programs by providing financial assistance for specific activities, entities, or groups of people. Because tax expenditures total over $1 trillion per year, constraining their total value could be a way to raise large amounts of revenue. One approach would be to eliminate most or all tax expenditures. Another approach would be to limit the amount of all or most tax expenditures—for example, to 28 percent of their total value. The staff of the Joint Committee on Taxation (JCT) has estimated, for example, that limiting the tax benefits of all itemized deductions and a broad set of other tax expenditures—such as the exclusion of most payments of premiums for employment-based health insurance—to 28 percent of their total value would increase revenues by over $400 billion from 2014 through 2023.

One rationale for eliminating or placing limits on tax expenditures is that many of those provisions—by effectively reducing the after-tax price of the preferred activities—lead to an inefficient allocation of economic resources because they encourage greater consumption of the goods and services receiving favored treatment than would occur without the tax preference. The home mortgage interest deduction, for example, not only encourages home ownership, it also encourages people to buy more expensive houses than they otherwise would purchase. However, some tax expenditures are intended to subsidize activities that have widespread benefits to the public, such as the work of charitable organizations that receive tax-subsidized contributions; under certain circumstances, curtailing the subsidy for those activities could worsen the allocation of resources.

Restrictions on tax expenditures would require trade-offs between policy goals. Some exclusions and deductions were created to achieve goals other than economic efficiency, such as lowering the after-tax costs of health insurance and higher education. The earned income tax credit and other refundable tax credits were designed to provide assistance to low- and moderate-income people that is not limited by the amount of tax owed in the absence of those tax credits. And although eliminating some tax expenditures would simplify tax returns, repealing others—such as the exclusion from taxable income of certain types of capital gains—would increase recordkeeping and paperwork for taxpayers. To address concerns about meeting various policy goals, lawmakers could choose to exclude some tax expenditures from limitation or elimination. However, such modifications would also lower the amount of additional revenues collected.

Continued

chose to mitigate some of the spending reductions that would occur under current law, the revenue increases would have to be even larger.

Many other objectives—either within the range defined by those approaches or outside of that range—are also

possible. Moreover, the size and scope of the government depend not just on the magnitude of total spending and revenues relative to GDP but also on the nature of spending programs and the tax code, the government's regulatory activities, and other factors. Tax expenditures, in particular, mask the true extent of government activity.

Imposing a Value-Added Tax

A value-added tax is a type of consumption tax that is collected at each stage of a good or service's production and distribution. A VAT has the potential of raising trillions of dollars over a 10-year period. Moreover, an advantage of creating a tax on consumption rather than increasing existing taxes on income is that such an approach would raise revenues without discouraging saving and investment. All the member countries of the Organisation for Economic Co-operation and Development except for the United States have adopted VATs.

However, a VAT would increase tax burdens on households and businesses and also add to the compliance burdens of businesses. One concern is that a comprehensive VAT would raise the cost of items commonly viewed as basic necessities, such as food, housing, and health care. In particular, because lower-income people consume a greater share of their income than wealthier people do, lower-income people would pay a larger percentage of their annual income through a comprehensive VAT than other people would. (Because families' incomes tend to fluctuate over time, VATs are somewhat less regressive over the long term.) Another concern is that a VAT would impose additional compliance costs on businesses, especially small businesses, because they would need to track both purchases and sales of goods and services.

Those concerns could be mitigated in several ways. For example, the VAT base could exclude goods that are viewed as necessities. Alternatively, transfer programs and refundable tax credits could be expanded to offset some of the effects of a VAT on lower-income households. As another example, to reduce compliance and administrative costs, lawmakers could exempt small businesses from the tax. However, each of those adjustments would diminish the amount of deficit reduction from a VAT.

Reducing the Tax Gap

Another approach to raising revenues is to improve the collection of taxes that are owed, but not paid, under current law. The Internal Revenue Service (IRS) estimates that the net tax gap—the amount of taxes owed but not collected (after accounting for revenues from enforcement actions and late payments)—was $385 billion in 2006, or about 15 percent of total tax liabilities. Most of that gap stems from the underreporting of income on tax returns. Efforts to reduce the tax gap, however, would impose additional costs—borne by taxpayers, the IRS, or both. For example, an increase in information reporting by taxpayers would enhance the IRS's ability to detect noncompliance but would raise taxpayers' costs of complying with the tax system. And the IRS might not be able to use those data without shifting resources from other initiatives (at some loss of current revenues from enforcement activities) or without an increase in its budget.

Because they appear in the budget as the absence of revenues that would otherwise be collected rather than as explicit spending, tax expenditures make the size of the budget and the scope of the government's activities appear smaller than they really are.[31]

Decisions about the size of the government would have significant consequences for the nation's ability to accom-

plish various goals. Under current law, the United States is on track to have a federal budget that will look very different from budgets of the past: As the population ages and health care costs rise, a much larger share of federal spending will go toward benefits for older people and a much smaller share will go toward other types of benefits and services, including government investments of various types. Over the long term, if federal spending for purposes other than Social Security, the major health care programs, and net interest matched what is projected in CBO's baseline, then the services that the government provides for national defense and for many nondefense

---

31. See Donald Marron and Eric Toder, *How Big Is the Federal Government?* Tax Policy Center (March 26, 2012), www.taxpolicycenter.org/publications/url.cfm?ID=412528.

Figure 5.

Components of Federal Spending Under CBO's Extended Baseline, 2013 and 2038

(Percentage of gross domestic product)

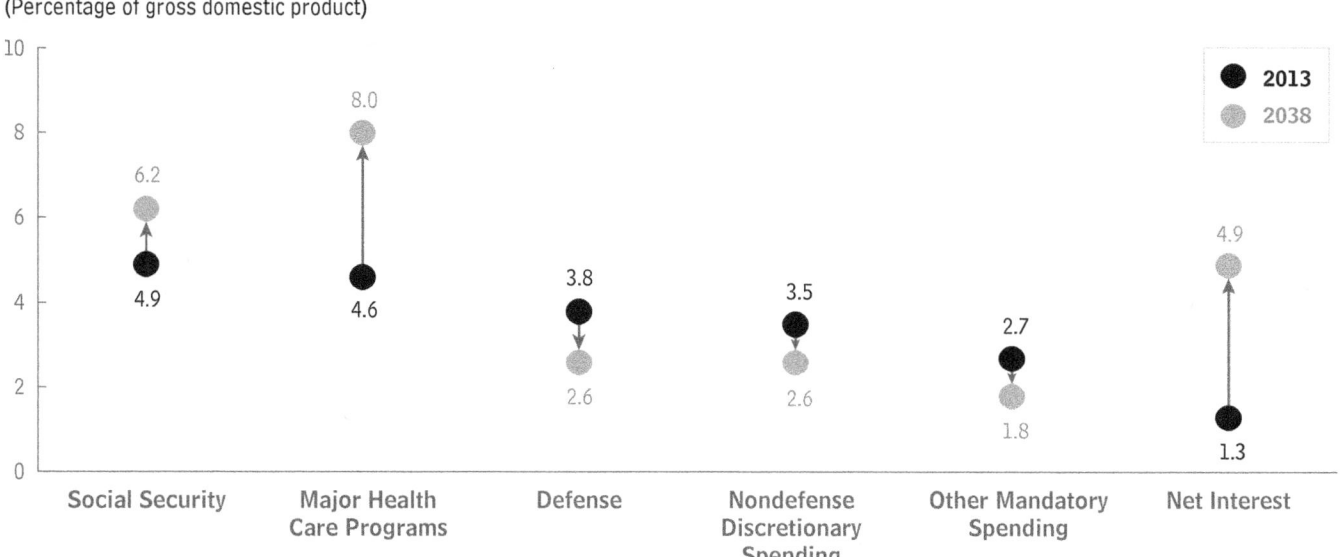

Source: Congressional Budget Office.

Notes: The extended baseline generally adheres closely to current law, following CBO's 10-year baseline budget projections through 2023 and then extending the baseline concept for the rest of the long-term projection period. See Congressional Budget Office, *The 2013 Long-Term Budget Outlook* (September 2013), www.cbo.gov/publication/44521.

These numbers reflect recent revisions by the Bureau of Economic Analysis to estimates of gross domestic product (GDP) in past years and CBO's extrapolation of those revisions to projected future GDP.

Numbers for 2013 were derived from information reported in Department of the Treasury, *Final Monthly Treasury Statement of Receipts and Outlays of the United States Government for Fiscal Year 2013 Through September 30, 2013, and Other Periods* (October 2013), www.fms.treas.gov/mts/mts0913.pdf.

Major health care programs consist of Medicare, Medicaid, the Children's Health Insurance Program, and subsidies offered through new health insurance exchanges. (Medicare spending is net of offsetting receipts.)

purposes—such as education, transportation, agriculture, and law enforcement—would shrink substantially compared with the output of other goods and services in the economy (see Figure 5). Significant reductions in total federal outlays relative to CBO's projections would require further reductions in such spending (relative to the size of the economy), a decrease in the benefits provided by Social Security and the health care programs, or both.

Changes to the tax code would also affect the government's impact on people's lives and the way in which federal resources are allocated to achieve various social goals. Higher taxes discourage the taxed activities and leave fewer resources for people to allocate for purposes that they choose themselves. Higher marginal tax rates (the percentage of an additional dollar of income from labor or capital that is subject to taxation) diminish people's incentives to work and save. If revenues were

increased by curtailing the number or size of deductions or credits in the tax system, the support that the government provides for various private activities through those tax preferences could be cut substantially.

How Much Would Deficits Be Reduced and How Quickly?

In considering policies aimed at reducing deficits, lawmakers would need to make judgments about how much deficit reduction should be accomplished in the next few years, the next 10 years, and subsequent decades. The amount of deficit reduction would depend on the amount of debt that lawmakers considered appropriate, and the timing of the reduction would depend on how lawmakers evaluated the trade-offs regarding the speed with which policies were changed.

The Amount of Deficit Reduction. To bring debt down to, say, 61 percent of GDP in 2023 would require reducing deficits by $2 trillion (excluding interest savings) over the next 10 years; extending to subsequent years the reduction in the deficit as a percentage of GDP in 2023 under this scenario would leave debt at 67 percent of GDP in 2038. Alternatively, to bring debt down to 51 percent of GDP in 2023—still above the percentage seen in any year between 1956 and 2008—would require reducing deficits by $4 trillion (excluding interest savings) over the next 10 years; extending to subsequent years the reduction in the deficit as a percentage of GDP in 2023 under this scenario would lower debt to 31 percent of GDP in 2038.

The changes in tax policies, spending policies, or both that would be needed to reach either of those targets for 2023 would be substantial. For instance, cutting deficits by $4 trillion (excluding interest savings) over the next decade relative to current law would require changes of the following sizes:

- If the deficit reduction was achieved entirely by cutting benefits from Social Security and major health care programs, those cuts would total 17 percent of the amount currently projected to be spent on those programs.

- If the deficit reduction was achieved entirely by cutting other noninterest spending (including spending for national defense), those cuts would total 22 percent of the amount currently projected to be spent on those programs.

- If the deficit reduction was achieved entirely through raising revenue, revenue collections would need to rise by 10 percent from currently projected amounts.

If the policy changes involved two of those three categories rather than just one, the changes would still need to be large. For example, if half of $4 trillion in deficit reduction stemmed from cuts to Social Security and major health care programs, and half came from increases in revenues, that combination would require a cut of 9 percent in spending for those programs and an increase of 5 percent in tax collections. All of those changes would be half as large if the deficit reduction target for the 2014–2023 period was $2 trillion.

Moreover, because the aging of the population and the continuing growth of health care costs would have budgetary consequences that extend well beyond the next 10 years, the fiscal challenges facing the nation are long-term in nature. CBO projects, in its extended baseline, that spending on the major federal health care programs alone would grow from about 4½ percent of GDP today to 8 percent in 25 years (see Figure 5). Spending on Social Security is projected to rise much less sharply, from about 5 percent of GDP today to more than 6 percent in 25 years.[32] Unless those programs are changed, or the increased spending is accompanied by some combination of sufficiently lower spending on other programs and sufficiently higher revenues, deficits would be much larger in the future than they have tended to be in the past.

Thus, to lower debt in the long term relative to CBO's extended baseline would require steps to reduce or constrain deficits beyond the next decade. Some policy options would have much greater budgetary effects after the next 10 years than they would during the next decade. For example, if an increase in the full retirement age for Social Security was phased in gradually or did not apply to people above a specified age threshold, it would have a much larger effect in future decades than in the next several years.[33] Similarly, if the growth rate of Medicare spending per beneficiary was effectively restrained through some policy change, the budgetary effects would compound over time, and the long-term savings would be much larger than the short-term savings. As another example, reducing people's initial Social Security benefits by 15 percent would cut spending by about 4 percent relative to the total benefits that would be paid under current law in 2023 but by about 12 percent relative to current-law benefits in 2038. Changes that reduced benefits in that way would have larger effects not only on future budget deficits but also on the future well-being of affected individuals.

The Timing of Deficit Reduction. Decisions about how quickly to reduce deficits involve difficult trade-offs. The longer that significant deficit reduction was deferred, the larger the government's accumulated debt—with its associated costs and risks—would be, and the greater the policy changes would need to be when deficit reduction began. Conversely, if the deficit was cut sooner rather

---

32. See Congressional Budget Office, *The 2013 Long-Term Budget Outlook* (September 2013), p. 11, www.cbo.gov/publication/ 44521.

33. For example, policy changes that excluded people who will be 55 or older in 2015 would not affect roughly 75 percent of baby boomers.

than later, households, businesses, and state and local governments would have little time to plan and adjust their behavior accordingly. Furthermore, policies that reduced deficits sharply in the next few years would lower output and income in those years relative to what they would otherwise be—reflecting the short-term impact of tax and spending policies on the demand for goods and services, especially under current economic conditions (as discussed in the next section).

What Would the Economic Impact Be?

Changes in federal tax and spending policies could have significant effects on the economy in both the short term and the long term—and the effects of a given change in policy could be quite different over those different time periods.

In the short term, changes in policies that decreased federal spending or raised taxes (and thus decreased budget deficits) would generally reduce demand, thereby lowering output and employment relative to what would otherwise occur. Alternatively, changes in policies that increased federal spending or cut taxes (and thus boosted budget deficits) would generally increase the demand for goods and services, thereby raising output and employment relative to what would occur in the absence of those policies. The magnitude of those effects would depend both on the specific changes in tax and spending policies and on economic conditions. The effects would tend to be especially strong under conditions like those currently prevailing in the United States, where output is so far below its potential (maximum sustainable) level that the Federal Reserve is keeping short-term interest rates near zero and probably would not adjust those rates to offset the effects of changes in federal spending and taxes.

By contrast, in the long term, changes in policies that decreased budget deficits would generally increase national saving and investment, thereby raising output and income relative to what would otherwise occur; changes in policies that increased budget deficits would generally have the opposite effects. Again, however, the economic effects would depend on the specific changes in tax and spending policies as well as on the magnitude of the change in deficits. In particular, the impact of changes in policies on people's incentives to work and save and on federal investment could affect the economic impact of any given change in deficits.

Impact in the Short Term. Under two illustrative scenarios that CBO has analyzed—in the first, the 10-year

deficit would be reduced by $2 trillion (excluding interest costs), and in the second, by $4 trillion—real GDP would be lower in the next several years than under current law, CBO estimates. The agency did not specify fiscal policies underlying the two illustrative scenarios, so the estimated economic effects arise solely from the differences in deficits:[34]

■ In the first scenario, CBO assumed that the deficit would be reduced gradually such that deficits (excluding interest costs) between fiscal years 2014 and 2023 would be $2 trillion less than those projected under current law; the reductions in the deficit (excluding interest costs) in fiscal years 2014 and 2015 were assumed to be $40 billion and $76 billion, respectively. Under this scenario, CBO estimates, real GDP in 2014 would be 0.2 percent lower than it is projected to be under current law, and real GDP in 2015 would be 0.3 percent lower.[35]

■ In the second scenario, CBO assumed that the deficit would be reduced gradually such that deficits (excluding interest costs) over the same period would be $4 trillion less than those projected under current law; the reductions in the deficit (excluding interest costs) in fiscal years 2014 and 2015 would amount to $80 billion and $151 billion, respectively. Under this scenario, CBO estimates, real GDP in 2014 would be 0.5 percent lower than it is projected to be under current law, and real GDP in 2015 would be 0.6 percent lower.

By CBO's estimates, real GDP under either scenario would stay below what it would be under current law for

---

34. Specifically, the projected outcomes under the scenarios reflect no direct changes to the incentives to work and save (such as changes in marginal tax rates or government benefit programs) or to federal investment. In fact, lessening budget deficits significantly relative to what would occur under current law without altering incentives to work and save or federal investment would be very difficult. If policies that lowered deficits affected those incentives or federal investment, then their overall economic impact would depend on both the changes in federal borrowing and the changes in incentives and federal investment.

35. Those results and others in this subsection are CBO's central estimates from ranges determined on the basis of alternative assumptions about how much reductions in taxes or increases in spending raise output and employment in the short run. For the full ranges and other information, see Congressional Budget Office, *The 2013 Long-Term Budget Outlook* (September 2013), www.cbo.gov/publication/44521.

a period after 2015, but would rise above what it would be under current law by 2018.[36] Because businesses would produce less in the next few years than under current law, they would hire fewer workers. Accordingly, CBO estimates that full-time-equivalent employment under the first of those scenarios would be 0.3 million lower in 2014 and 0.4 million lower in 2015 than employment under current law and that full-time-equivalent employment under the second of those scenarios would be 0.5 million lower in 2014 and 0.8 million lower in 2015 than employment under current law.

Impact in the Long Term. In the long term, a reduction in federal borrowing relative to what would occur under current law would increase the stock of private capital (such as factories, vehicles, and computers) and thereby raise output and income relative to what they would be otherwise. Consider the same illustrative scenarios:

■ In the first scenario, CBO assumed that the reduction in the deficit in 2023 as a percentage of GDP is continued in subsequent years. CBO projects that real gross national product (GNP) would be 0.8 percent higher in 2023 and about 4 percent higher in 2038 under that scenario than under current law.[37]

■ In the second scenario, which involves greater deficit reduction, CBO assumed that the reduction in the deficit in 2023 as a percentage of GDP also is continued in subsequent years. CBO projects that real GNP would be 1.6 percent higher in 2023 and about 7 percent higher in 2038 under that scenario than under current law.

Because CBO did not specify fiscal policies underlying the two illustrative scenarios, the estimated economic effects arise solely from the differences in deficits. The

specific policy changes used to achieve the assumed reduction in federal borrowing could have other effects on future output and income as well.

For example, increasing revenues by raising marginal tax rates on labor would reduce people's incentive to work and therefore reduce the amount of labor supplied to the economy, whereas increasing revenues to a similar extent by broadening the tax base would probably have a smaller negative effect, or even a positive effect, on the amount of labor supplied.[38] A reduction in the labor supply, by itself, would decrease output in the long term. Similarly, increasing marginal tax rates on capital would tend to reduce people's incentive to save and thus the amount of private saving, which would also decrease output in the long term (excluding the effects of less federal borrowing). Alternatively, on the spending side, cutting government benefit payments, such as unemployment insurance or retirement benefits, would probably strengthen people's incentives to work and save, although the impact would depend on the nature of the cuts. Another approach, reducing federal investment in such things as infrastructure and education, would decrease future output (also excluding the effects of less federal borrowing).

Therefore, to assess the overall economic impact of a deficit reduction plan in the long term, the favorable effects of less federal borrowing must be combined with the effects of the specific changes in taxes and spending.[39] However, even if lawmakers reduced federal budget deficits through policy changes that worsened incentives to work and save and that trimmed federal investment, the

36. See Congressional Budget Office, *The 2013 Long-Term Budget Outlook* (September 2013), Chapter 6, www.cbo.gov/publication/ 44521.

37. Those results and others in this subsection are CBO's central estimates from ranges determined on the basis of alternative assumptions about how much deficits "crowd out" investment in capital goods such as factories and computers (because a larger portion of people's savings is being used to purchase government securities). Unlike the more commonly cited GDP, GNP includes the income that U.S. residents earn abroad and excludes the income that foreigners earn in this country; GNP is therefore a better measure of the resources available to U.S. households.

38. Broadening the tax base would have opposing effects on labor supply. On the one hand, reducing taxpayers' after-tax income would tend to cause them to work more to make up for the loss in income. On the other hand, some approaches for broadening the tax base would raise some taxpayers' marginal tax rates—by pushing those taxpayers into higher tax brackets, for example— which would tend to cause the taxpayers to work less. Whether the net effect was positive or negative would depend on the details of the policy change.

39. See the testimony of Douglas W. Elmendorf, Director, Congressional Budget Office, before the Joint Select Committee on Deficit Reduction, *Confronting the Nation's Fiscal Policy Challenges* (September 2011), pp. 43–47, www.cbo.gov/ publication/42761. For a discussion of the methods that CBO uses to assess such effects, see Congressional Budget Office, *The Economic Impact of the President's 2013 Budget* (April 2012), pp. 13–18, www.cbo.gov/publication/42972.

net impact on the nation's long-term output and income would probably be positive.[40]

To the extent that deficit reduction led to greater output and income in the long term, the deficit would be reduced further through higher revenues. In addition, the decrease in federal borrowing would lower interest rates, which would cut the government's interest payments. Thus, somewhat smaller policy changes would be needed to achieve any particular target for deficit reduction than calculations that exclude such macroeconomic effects would imply. However, the additional deficit reduction that would result from those economic effects would probably be small relative to the more direct impact of the policy changes. Specifically, CBO has estimated that the increase in taxable income and the reduction in interest rates that would result from a gradual decrease in deficits over the coming decade would generate additional deficit reduction that would be about 5 percent of the size of the reduction in deficits excluding interest costs over that period resulting directly from policy changes.[41]

Some policymakers have proposed broadly restructuring the individual income tax system, the corporate income tax system, or both, either as part of an effort to reduce deficits or as an effort to make those systems simpler, fairer, or more efficient. If such restructuring strengthened the economy in the long term, it would increase taxable income and thereby reduce deficits. As an illustration, suppose that tax restructuring lowered the effective marginal tax rate on labor earnings by 5 percentage points. Suppose also that the revenue loss was made up exactly—without incorporating any macroeconomic effects—by expanding the tax base. According to a rough estimate by CBO, the resulting increase in GDP would probably boost tax revenues by less than half of 1 percent of GDP by the end of the coming decade.[42] Changes to the tax code that reduced effective marginal tax rates to a lesser extent and also had no net impact on deficits in the absence of any macroeconomic effects would generally

have smaller effects on GDP and tax revenues. However, the impact of any particular plan for restructuring the tax system would depend not only on the size of changes in marginal tax rates but also on the distribution of those changes among taxpayers and any other effects of the restructuring on the allocation of resources in the economy.

Who Would Bear the Burden of Proposed Changes in Tax and Spending Policies?

Different types of tax increases and spending cuts would affect various groups of people to different extents. Those effects could be direct, such as changes in the amount of taxes that people owed or the amount of benefits or services they received, or indirect, such as changes that altered the state of the economy. Indirect effects are harder to anticipate because they depend on the behavior of many different participants in the economy.

Most changes in taxes and spending programs would affect how tax burdens and government benefits and services were distributed among people at different income levels. In addition, many such changes would alter the relative tax burdens of, and benefits received by, people who have similar income but who differ in other ways. Policy changes might also influence the distribution of taxes and spending across generations.

CBO recently analyzed how tax burdens and government benefits and services were distributed among the population in 2006, the most recent year for which sufficient data were available. The combined effect of federal

---

40. For an analysis of one such scenario, see the testimony of Douglas W. Elmendorf, Director, Congressional Budget Office, before the Senate Committee on the Budget, *The Economic Outlook and Fiscal Policy Choices* (September 2010), www.cbo.gov/publication/21836.

41. See Congressional Budget Office, *The Macroeconomic Effects of Alternative Budgetary Paths* (February 2013), www.cbo.gov/publication/43769.

42. Lowering the effective marginal tax rate on labor earnings by 5 percentage points would require a larger reduction in statutory tax rates because some forms of compensation are excluded from taxable income and because some options for broadening the tax base increase people's taxable income and thereby push some of them into higher tax brackets. CBO's reading of the evidence about how the supply of labor responds to changes in tax rates suggests that such a substantial cut in the tax rate would probably increase the labor supply by 2 percent or less; see Congressional Budget Office, *How the Supply of Labor Responds to Changes in Fiscal Policy* (October 2012), www.cbo.gov/publication/43674. Tax restructuring could also boost the capital stock by reducing the effective marginal tax rate on capital income, which would encourage saving, and by generating higher earnings by workers, which would also boost saving. If those effects together increased the long-term capital stock by an amount comparable to the increase in the labor supply, GDP would rise by 2 percent or less. An increase in GDP of that magnitude would boost federal tax revenues by less than half of 1 percent of GDP.

Figure 6.

Average Transfers, Taxes, and Transfers Minus Taxes per Household, by Type of Household, 2006

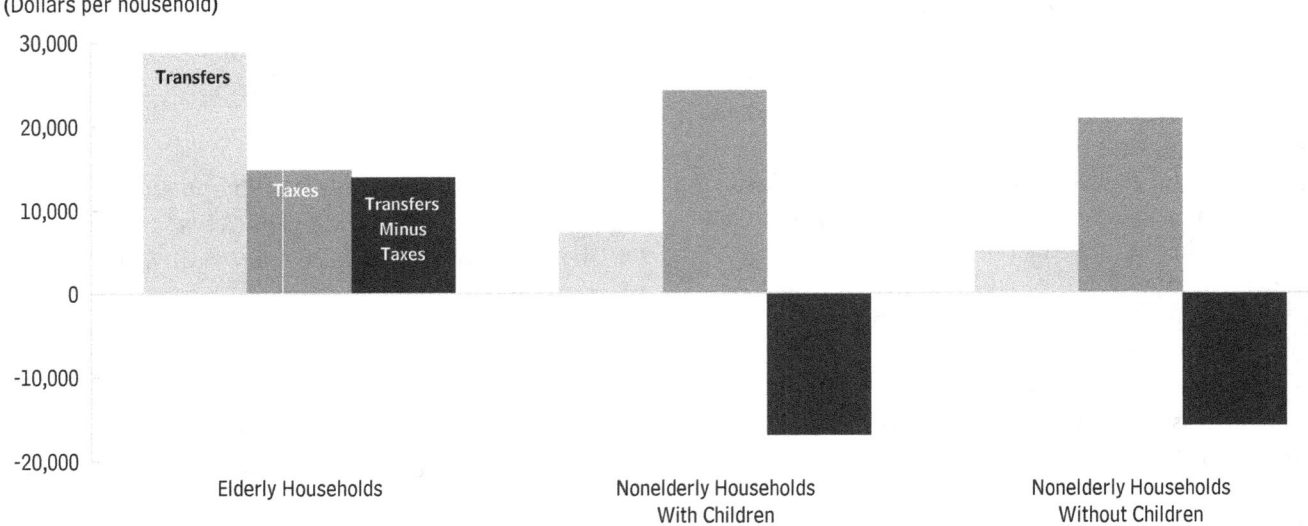

(Dollars per household)

Source: Congressional Budget Office.

Note: Transfers are benefits from government assistance—such as from Social Security, Medicare, and Medicaid—which together accounted for 48 percent of federal spending in 2006. Taxes made up 98 percent of federal revenues in that year. Households (consisting of people who share a housing unit, regardless of their relationships) are categorized as elderly when a person who owns or rents the unit is age 65 or older.

transfers and taxes is to shift resources from people living in nonelderly households to people living in elderly households and to shift resources from higher-income nonelderly households to lower-income nonelderly households. Specifically, CBO estimated the following:

■ In 2006, average transfer payments to elderly households, almost entirely through Social Security and Medicare, were nearly twice as large as average taxes paid by that group. In contrast, nonelderly households in that year paid significantly more in taxes, on average, than they received in transfers (see Figure 6).[43]

■ Among nonelderly households in the lowest income quintile, average market income was roughly $13,000 in 2006 compared with about $240,000 for households in the highest income quintile.[44] (Each of those quintiles represents one-fifth of the population living in nonelderly households.) The combined effect of taxes and transfers narrowed that difference a little,

as average income after taxes and transfers was roughly $25,000 for the bottom fifth and $175,000 for the top fifth.

■ Half of spending on federal transfers for nonelderly households in 2006 was for people in the lowest 20 percent of the income distribution (see Figure 7). Moreover, people in nonelderly households in the lowest 20 percent of the income distribution paid only about 2 percent of the taxes paid by nonelderly households in that year.

■ The share of taxes paid by households in the highest 20 percent of the distribution was roughly 65 percent. The large share of taxes paid by nonelderly households with higher income was a result of both their large share of market income in that year (roughly

---

43. See Congressional Budget Office, *The Distribution of Federal Spending and Taxes in 2006* (November 2013), www.cbo.gov/publication/44698.

44. In this study, households were ranked by their market income, which consists of labor income, business income, capital gains, capital income (excluding capital gains), and other sources of nontransfer income. The total market income for each household was then adjusted to account for differences in the number of people in each household.

Figure 7.

Average Transfers, Taxes, and Transfers Minus Taxes for Nonelderly Households, by Income Group, 2006

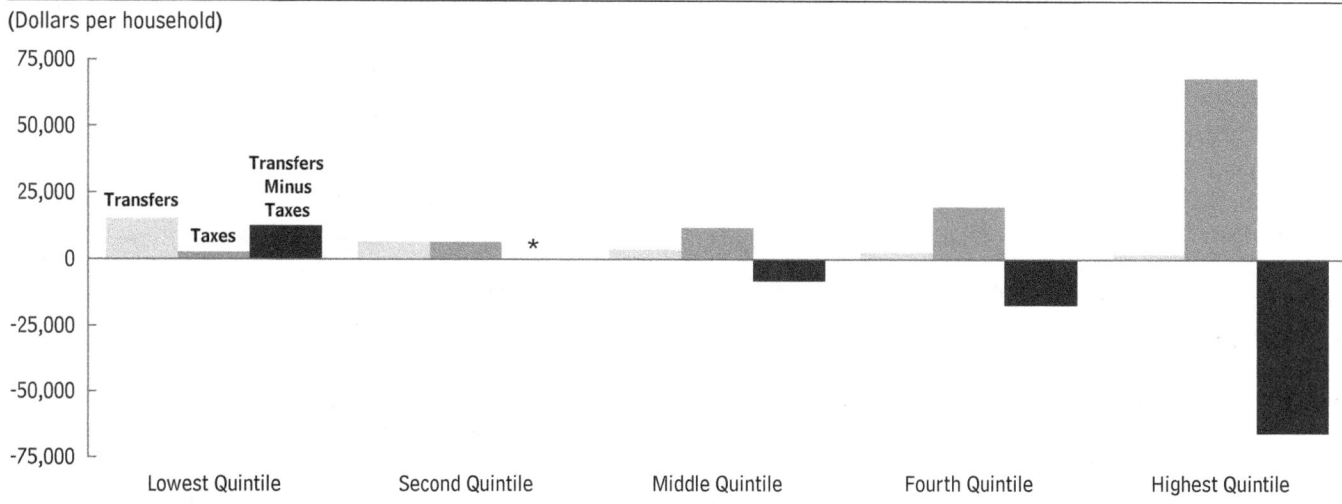

(Dollars per household)

Source: Congressional Budget Office.

Notes: Transfers are benefits from government assistance, such as from Social Security, Medicare, and Medicaid; transfers to nonelderly households together accounted for 21 percent of federal spending in 2006. Taxes paid by nonelderly households made up 83 percent of federal revenues in that year.

Nonelderly households are ranked by their annual market income, which was adjusted for household size by dividing income by the square root of the number of people in the household, and grouped into quintiles (or fifths) containing equal numbers of people. (Elderly households are not included here.) Market income consists of labor income, business income, capital gains, capital income (excluding capital gains), and other nontransfer income.

* = between zero and $500.

55 percent) and the progressivity of the federal tax system, which results in tax payments representing a larger share of income for households with higher income.

Based on data for income and tax collections through 2010, CBO finds that the distribution of federal taxes shifted somewhat after 2006, reflecting changes both in tax rules and in economic conditions.[45] Between 2006 and 2010, average federal tax rates (taxes divided by household income) fell for households in all income groups but by larger amounts for households in the lower income quintiles than for households in the higher income quintiles. Consequently, the shares of federal taxes paid by households in the highest two quintiles rose,

while the shares paid by the lower three quintiles fell. Changes in tax rules since 2010 have raised average federal tax rates for all income groups, with larger increases for households in the top percentile of the income distribution.

Policy changes that increased revenues would probably affect the distribution of the tax burden, but the effects would depend on the type of tax raised and the nature of the increase. Raising income tax rates for higher-income people would make the tax system more progressive. By contrast, increasing most excise taxes—such as those on tobacco or gasoline—would boost the relative tax burdens of lower-income people, who tend to spend a greater proportion of their income on those items. Alternatively, taxes could be raised in such a way as to roughly maintain the current distribution of the tax burden.

Cuts in spending programs would also affect households differently depending on their income. For example, reducing benefits in the Supplemental Nutrition Assistance Program would increase burdens on the program's

---

45. For more details, see Congressional Budget Office, *The Distribution of Household Income and Federal Taxes, 2010* (December 2013), www.cbo.gov/publication/44604. That study ranked households by their before-tax income, which includes both market income and government transfers, and considered both elderly and nonelderly households together.

beneficiaries, who have low income. As another example, raising the full retirement age for Social Security would reduce people's lifetime benefits and would be particularly burdensome for recipients with low income, who tend to rely heavily on Social Security benefits. Such a policy change could be especially difficult for people who could not adjust their work patterns or qualify for Social Security Disability Insurance benefits in response to the change. Other cuts in government benefits or services could have different effects on people with lower or higher income.

Some policy changes that would reduce deficits would affect people with similar income differently. For instance, reducing or eliminating the child tax credit would lessen the economic well-being of people who have dependent children compared with that of people at similar income levels who do not; and eliminating the deduction for state and local taxes would increase tax payments more for people who live in states with high taxes. As another example, some observers gauge the fairness of highway spending by considering the share of funding that comes from taxes paid by highway users rather than from general taxpayer funds or the share of funding that comes from people in rural versus urban areas.

Policy changes can also be evaluated in terms of how they would affect different generations. Deficit reduction policies that took effect now would generally increase burdens on people living today. Depending on the specific policy choices, future generations might also receive fewer government benefits and services or pay higher taxes; in some cases, those effects could be greater than the effects on current generations. However, future generations would also benefit from a larger economy and greater income in the long term if deficits were lower than would otherwise be the case.

List of Tables and Figures